THE POET and the CALLIGRAPHER

With thanks to Isabelle Massoudy for selecting the verses
contained herein, and for all her support since my first
book was published in 1981. Every work is a collaboration.

Published 2025 by Saqi Books

ISBN 978 1 84925 077 1
eISBN 978 1 84925 078 8

The EU GPSR authorised representative is
Logos Europe, 9 rue Nicolas Poussin, 17000 La Rochelle, France.
E-mail: Contact@logoseurope.eu

A full CIP record for this book is available from the British Library.

Printed by PBtisk s.a.

SAQI
Gable House, 18–24 Turnham Green Terrace, London W4 1QP
www.saqibooks.com

HASSAN MASSOUDY

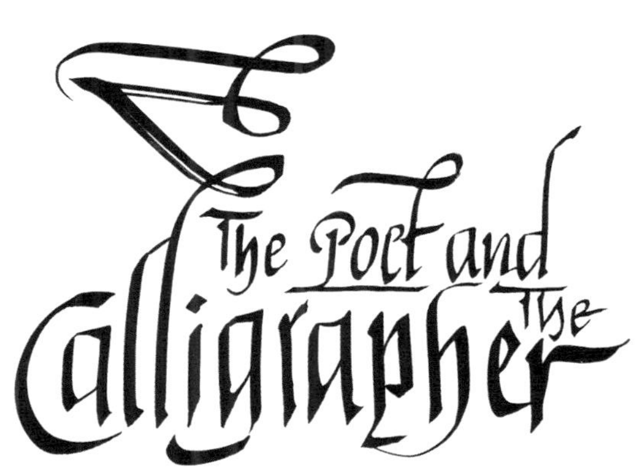

SAQI

INTRODUCTION

A bond is created between the calligrapher and the poet. The calligrapher transforms the words of the poet, leading them down another path, giving them new life. The calligrapher uses poetry to build their composition, making letters fly, mixing, curving and bending words to their will. A calligrapher is the choreographer of letters. They make words dance. They strive to create osmosis between form and meaning. But sometimes a letter, word or phrase resists and refuses to obey the calligrapher's quill. The calligrapher tries over again to capture the essence of a word. At times, the calligrapher may betray the poet, but the poet is indispensable to the calligrapher.

The foundations of Arabic poetry can be traced back to the pre-Islamic poets of Arabia. These poets lived in the desert and their poems evoked the immensity and the infinite time and space of their home, alongside tales of the departure of the tribe to other camps and lost love. Each tribe had its own poet, who was the guarantor of the tribe's memory and told its story like an epic. As pre-Islamic poetry was oral, the poets chiselled their poems like jewels, using simple words and a sober style. This suits the calligrapher well, who prefers short verses that have the ability to instantly conjure an image that the calligrapher can translate into a gesture or line on paper or canvas.

When the pre-Islamic Arabs were expressing themselves through poetry, calligraphy was still in its infancy. Poetry was central to the future development of Arabic calligraphy, for both forms served to magnify one another. At times, they also serve to obscure one another's meaning.

Like the calligrapher who plays with letters, the poet does not directly reveal the meaning of each word. They invite the listener or reader to become involved by interpreting their work as they wish, in accordance with their own desires. A poem or piece of art can be a vehicle for the listener or reader to express their innermost feelings and navigate the depths of their own soul. In this way, the poet's words merge with the ideas of the reader, depending on their own personal experiences.

When I talk about calligraphy, I like to use the term image. Writing was born from images. The ancient Sumerian and Egyptian scripts were comprised of simplified images, just like all the letters of the alphabet to come. Calligraphy is the quintessence of images: images that are original, not natural or photographic; images that emerge as signs. From this idea of symbolic images to express language, the need to calligraphy texts arose. I choose literary texts that are capable of withstanding the process of being broken down and reconstructed. This is how Arabic poetry came to dominate my artistic practice. Poets enrich me with their visions, ideas and feelings. Poetry offers a freedom of visual expression, of dreaming, as illustrated by its ability to both deconstruct and reconstruct words.

It is necessary to start each new calligraphy by first visualising the shapes of the letters. Next, the calligrapher develops the structure as an immense sculpture, starting from the ground and rising towards the sky, creating a new

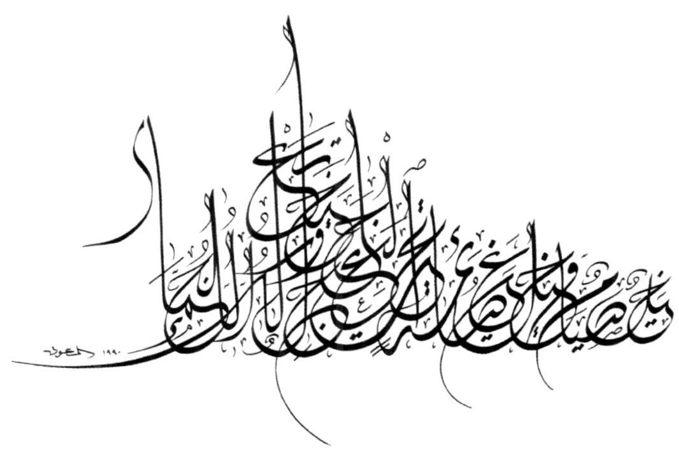

Horses with hollow bellies
Horses satiated by the wind of the sands
Horses gnawing impatiently at their bits.

al-Nabiga al-Dubyani (535–604)

خيل صيام ، وخيل غير صائمة ،
تحت العجاج ، وأخرى تعلك اللجما.
النابغة الذبياني

composition. The calligrapher must consider the rising letters as both resisting the atmospheric pressure of the air and the gravitational pull of the Earth. The actual size of calligraphic creation is irrelevant, because even if it is small, the work reflects a larger image.

Arabic calligraphy is inspired by nature without imitating it. It is directly linked to its geometric and rhythmic properties. Certain compositions are also influenced by the architecture of the structure on which they will be integrated. The calligrapher who executes his compositions on monuments will charge the letters with visual energy, paying attention to the width of the wall inscriptions and the variety of colours or motifs applied alongside the letters to create an impression of depth.

A calligrapher must strive to produce the most beautiful letters, down to the smallest details. If the calligrapher is not at their best, the weakness of the letters and the fragility of the structure will reveal this. Above all, the calligrapher should seek a calm environment and, before starting, spend long hours practicing the whole alphabet in the style of their choice.

I calligraphy texts for their aesthetic appeal rather than for reading. My calligraphies derive their importance from the geometric shapes, not their meaning. This aesthetic desire leads me to reorganise letters or words into groups, bringing similar letters together and wrapping them around each other, while separating incompatible ones and reducing their size. The calligraphy then creates a geometric structure based on the vertical forms of certain letters and others that are more curvilinear and rounded. Sometimes, the letters look serene and motionless, sometimes they seem dynamic and determined. They fly back and forth, hesitantly or determinedly, expressing anger or joy. Every time two or three letters meet, a new shape emerges. The shape of the space between letters is essential. White is as important as black or colour. Managing the void is as important as managing the words themselves.

Calligraphic composition should be seen as a whole. Words and letters should not be examined or read independently. The letters must be seen together and assessed purely on their aesthetic aspect, like contemplating a tree as a whole, without focusing only on its branches or leaves. The shape must convey a vision of geometric balance and harmony, through the interlaced calligraphic strokes, the lightness or weight of the letters and the space that surrounds them. In Arabic script, the shape of a letter differs according to its position in the word, but on occasion, this rule does not apply in calligraphy. It is the final structure that matters, achieved by grouping letters together or changing their shape. Each sentence, group of words or letters can be arranged in different ways. This is why several interpretations of the same sentence are possible, depending on the inspiration of the day, the mood, the colour of time, the style of writing and, above all, the texts of a poet one particularly likes. For example, I have calligraphed certain phrases of ibn Zaydun, the great Andalusian poet, hundreds of times and each one is unique.

One must be aware of the heritage of ancient calligraphers and build a bridge between the classical and modern writings. Once I had familiarised myself with classical calligraphy, I had to forget everything I had learned to attempt to create contemporary calligraphy. Otherwise, it would be impossible to express my feelings or open the door to new ideas. If I want my calligraphy to reflect the present moment, with the precision and perfection I strive for, I must draw it quickly. Some people may be apprehensive about this new approach, feeling it to be unfamiliar. But over time, change becomes part of the tradition. Calligraphic traditions await the arrival of new creators who will add their own stylistic innovations to the journey.

The poet is the prince of words, the calligrapher the choreographer.

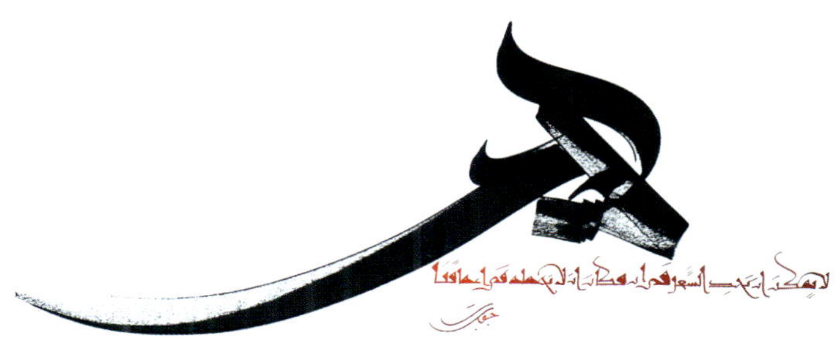

Poetry is the font of Arab knowledge
Book of their wisdom
Record of their tidings
Repository of their days
A wall built upon their deeds
A trench reserved for their glories
Fair witness on day of renunciation
Decisive proof in times of dispute
Of poetry, much has been said.

Ibn Qutaybah (828–886)

الشّعرُ معدنُ علم العرب
وسِفَر حكمتها
وديوانُ أخبارها
ومستودعُ أيّامها
والسّورُ المضروب على مآثرها
والخندقُ المحجوز على مفاخرها
والشّاهدُ العدل يوم النّفار
والحجّةُ القاطعة عند الخصام
وما جاء في الشّعر كثير...

ابن قتيبة

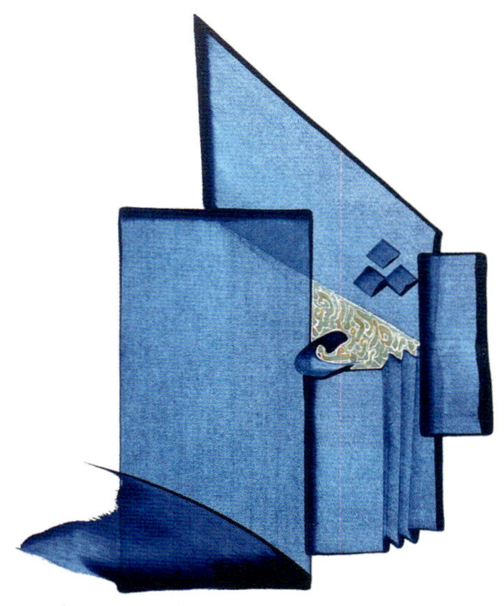

◀ ▶ Poetry cannot be found
anywhere, if one doesn't
carry it inside.

Joseph Joubert (1754–1824)

لا يمكن ان نجد الشعر
في أي مكان
ان لم نحمله في اعماقنا.
جوزيف جوبرت

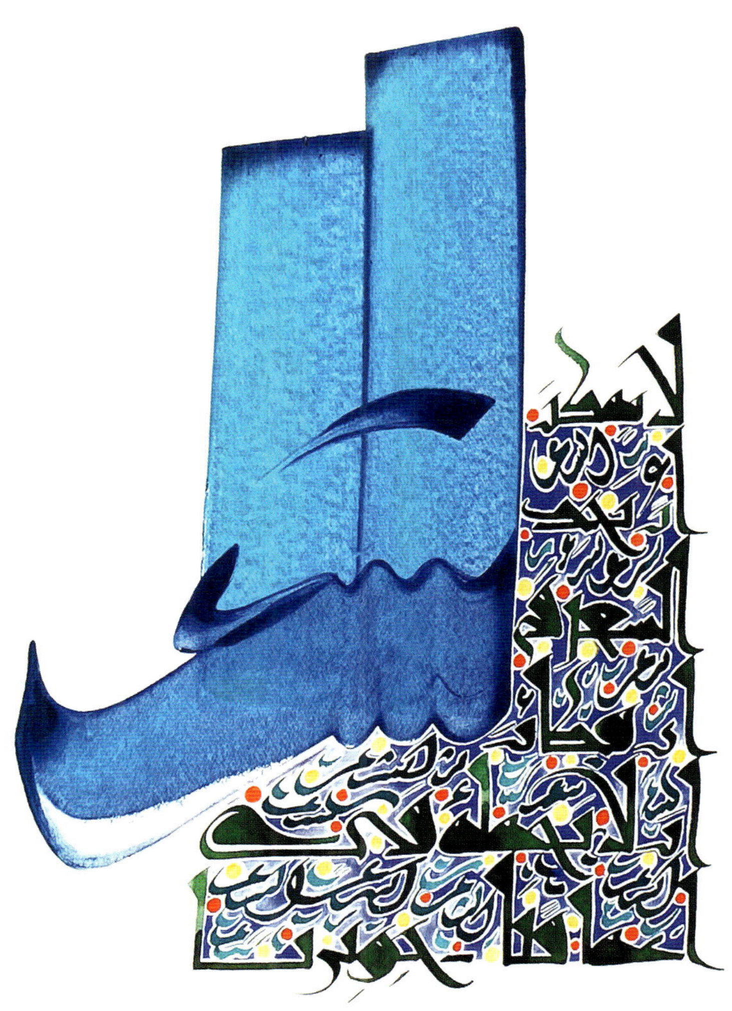

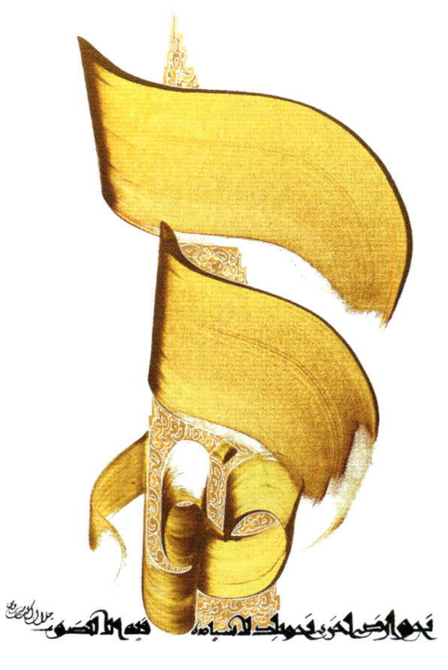

Towards another land, a country
where only light reigns.

Jalal al-Din Rumi (1207–1273)

نحو أرضٍ أخرى، نحو بلدٍ لا سيادة فيه
إلّا للنّور.

جلال الدين الرومي

Your heart knows the way, run in its direction.

Jalal al-Din Rumi

قلبك يعرف الطّريق؛ اركضْ بهذا الاتّجاه.

جلال الدين الرومي

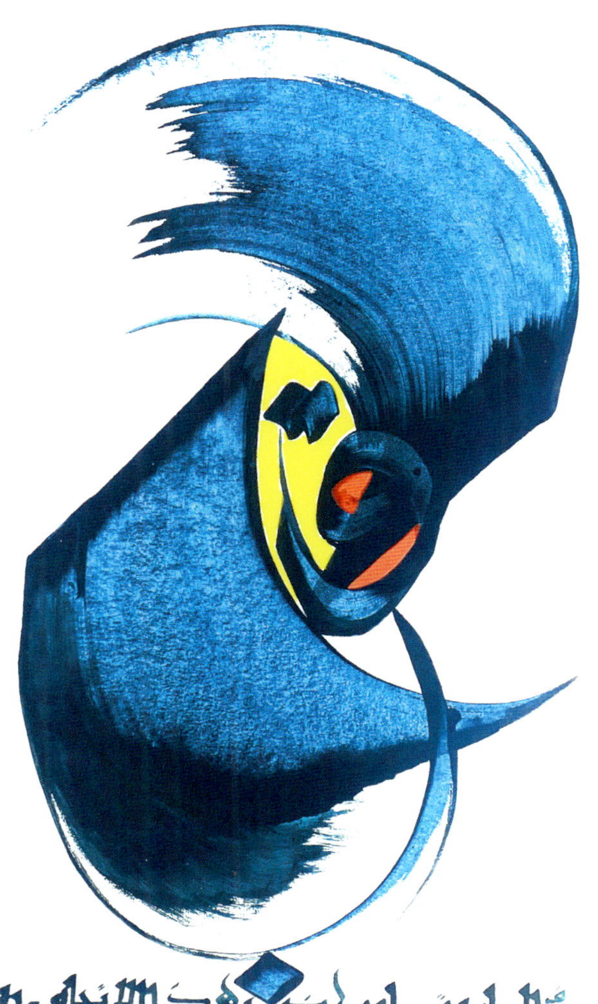

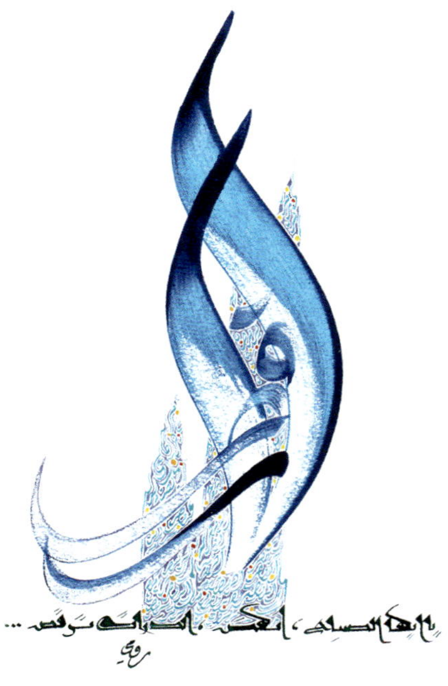

Never lose hope, my heart,
miracles dwell in the invisible.

Shams Tabrizi (1185–1248)

يا قلب، لا تفقد الأمل،
فالمعجزات تختبىء فيما لا نراه.
شمس التبريزي

O day, arise, the atoms dance
Souls dance for joy, without head or feet.
He for whom the firmament and the atmosphere dance
I'll tell you where the dance takes him.

Jalal al-Din Rumi (1207–1273)

يا أيّها الصّباح، انهض، الذرّات ترقص...
جلال الدين الرومي

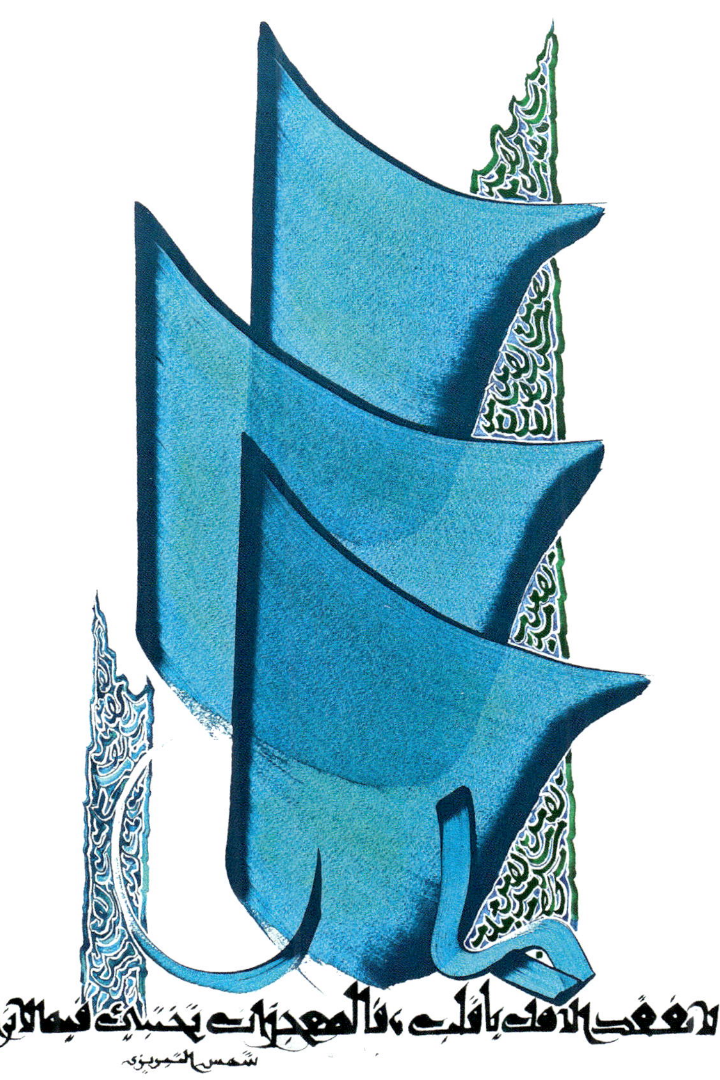

وامعد الملك يأتيك، فالمعجزات يحسبك فيما لايراه
شمس الشويزي

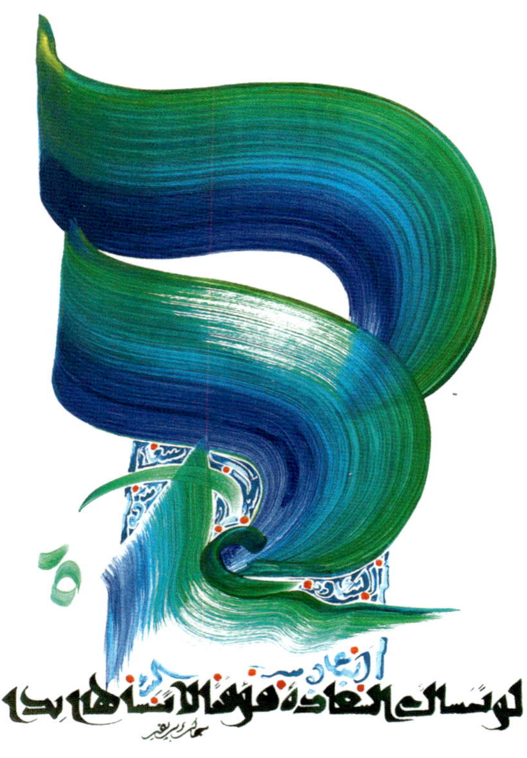

▲ ▶

Even if happiness forgets you occasionally, never forget it completely.

Jacques Prévert (1900–1977)

لو تنساك السّعادة مؤقّتاً، لا تنسَها أبداً.

جاك بريفير

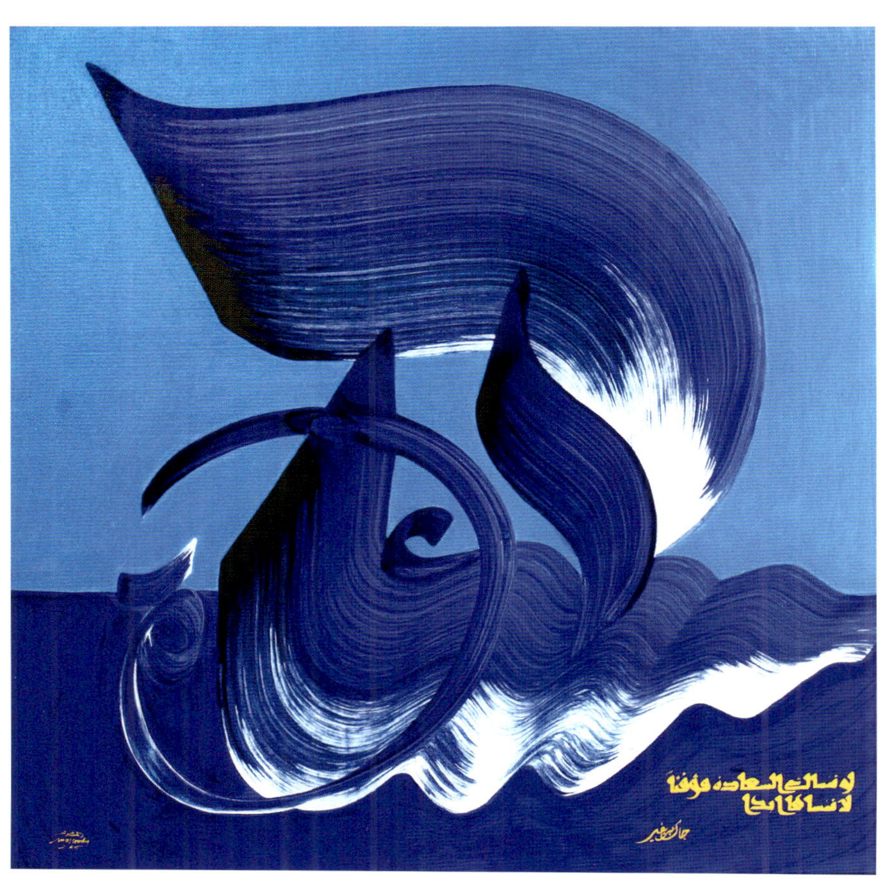
و نسائي السعادة فوقنا
لأنسانا أخا

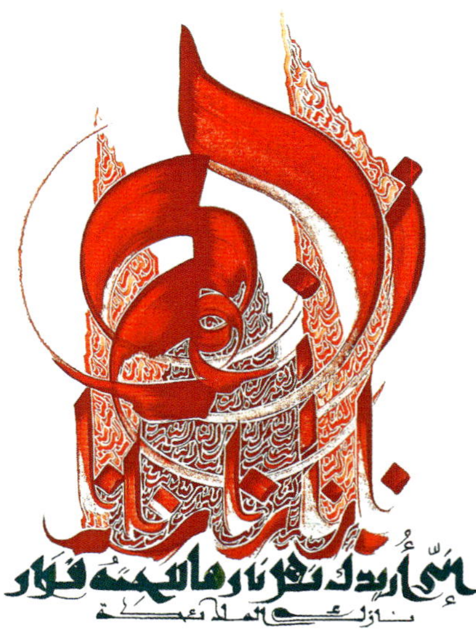

◂

I want you as a bottomless river
bursting with flame.

Nazik al-Mala'ika (1923–2007)

إنّي أريدك نهر نار
ما للجته قرار.
نازك الملائكة

▸

I, like the volcano's thirst for eruption, the deep
night's fierce desire for a meeting with the day, the
overflowing spring's wish to be held in jars of clay,
I want you as a bottomless river bursting with flame
becomes mad and curses death as sick of the dead.

Nazik al-Mala'ika

إنّي أحبّ تعطّش البركان فيك إلى انفجار.
نازك الملائكة

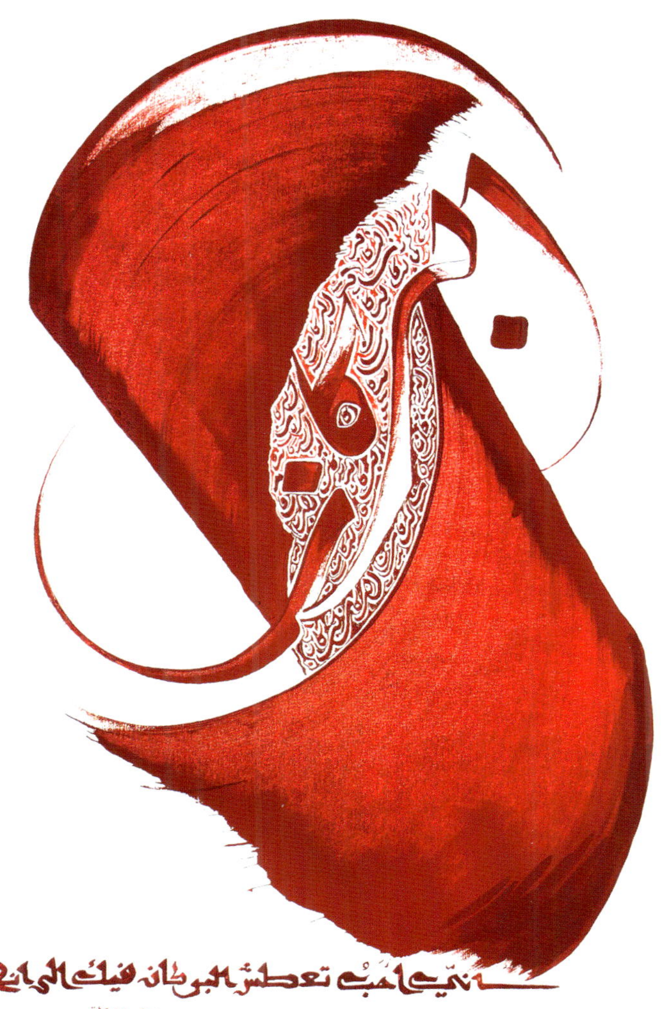

سنريهم آياتنا في الآفاق وفي أنفسهم حتى يتبين لهم أنه الحق

The night asks who am I?
I am its secret – anxious, black, profound
I am its rebellious silence
I have veiled my nature with silence
wrapped my heart in doubt
and, solemn, remained here
gazing, while the ages ask me,
who am I?

The wind asks who am I?
I am its confused spirit, whom time has disowned
I, like it, never resting
continue to travel without end
continue to pass without pause.
Should we reach a bend
we would think it the end of our suffering
and then – void.

Nazik al-Mala'ika (1923–2007)

اللّيل يسأل من أنا
أنا سرُّه القلق العميق الأسودُ
أنا صمتُه المتمرّدُ.
نازك الملائكة

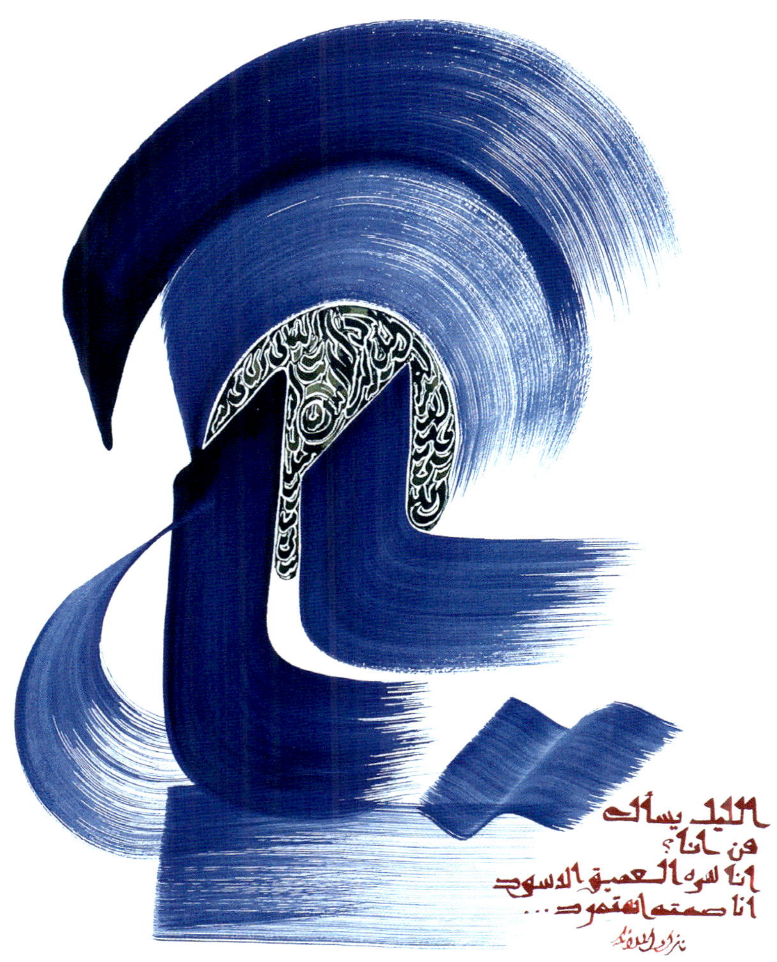

الليل يسألك
من أنا؟
أنا سره العميق الأسود
أنا صمته المتمرد...
نزار قباني

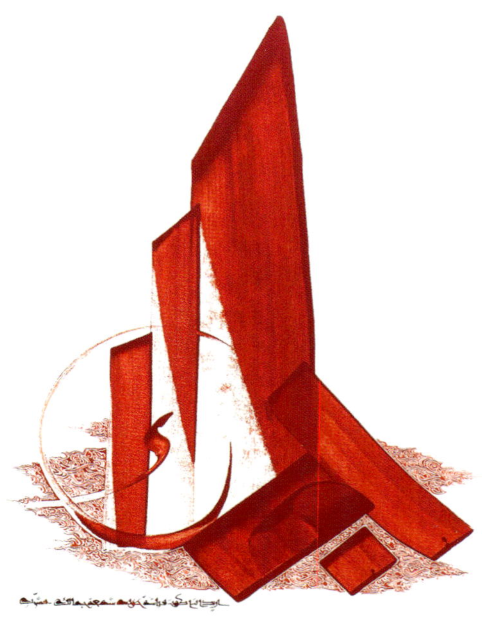

I wish to be a butterfly flying around the
candle of your beauty.

Mashrab (1651–1711)

أريد أن أكون فراشة حول شمعة جمالك.

مشرب

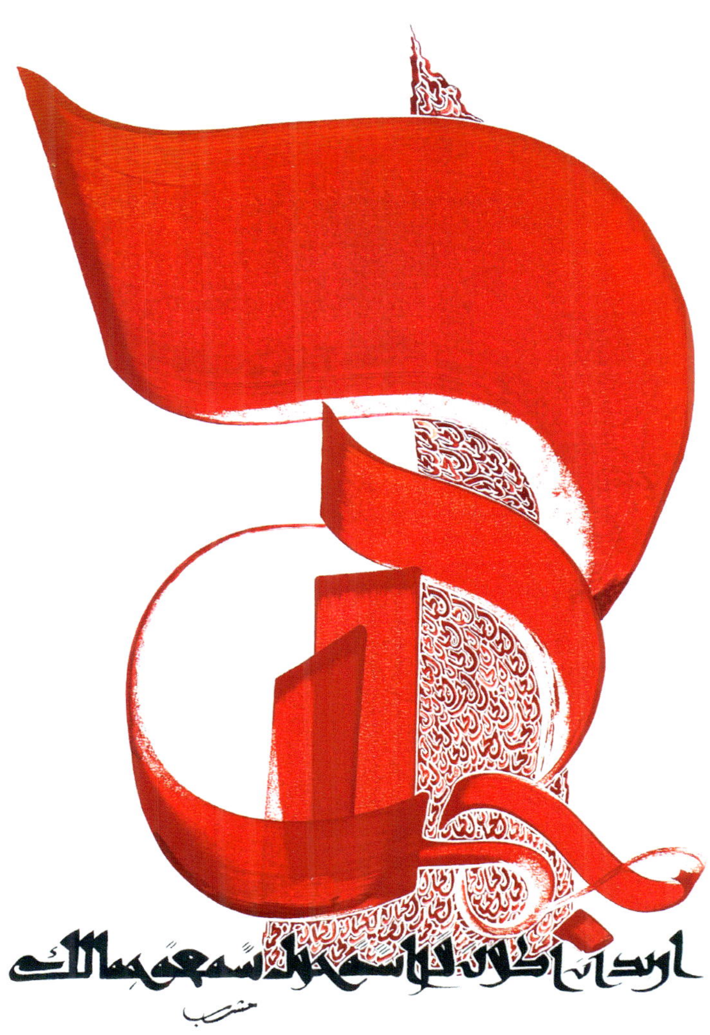

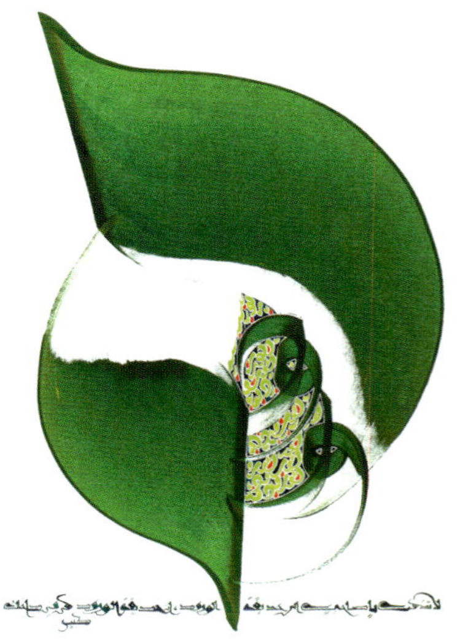

▲ ►

Don't go to the flower garden!
O friend, don't go there,
Within you is the garden of flowers.
Abide on the lotus of a thousand petals
And there contemplate infinite Beauty.

Kabir (1440–1518)

لا تذهب ياصاحبي الى حديقة الزهور
ان حديقة الزهور هي في داخلك
كبير

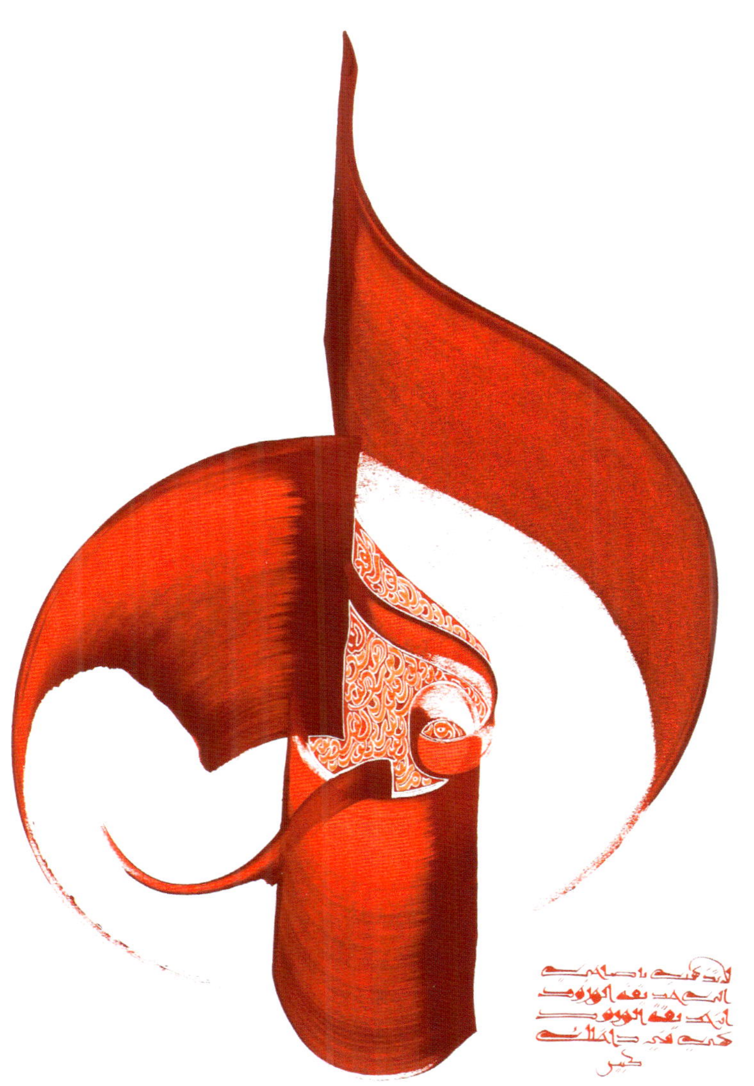

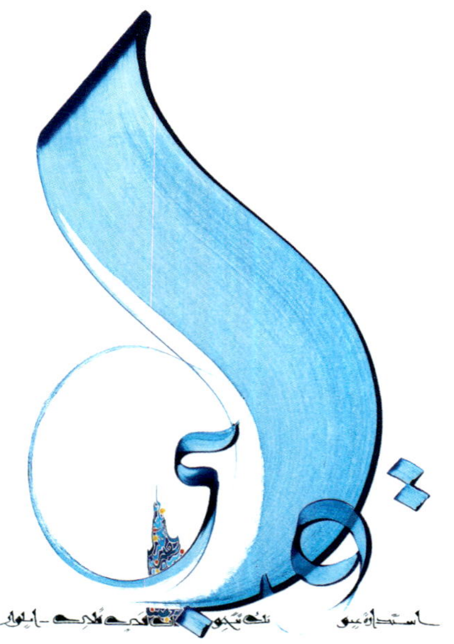

▲ ▶

The curve of your eyes circles my heart,
A circle of dance and sweetness,
An aureole of time, a safe night cradle,
And if I no longer know everything I've lived through
It's because your eyes haven't always seen me.

Paul Éluard (1895–1952)

استدارة عينيْك تتجوّل في قلبي.

بول إيلوار

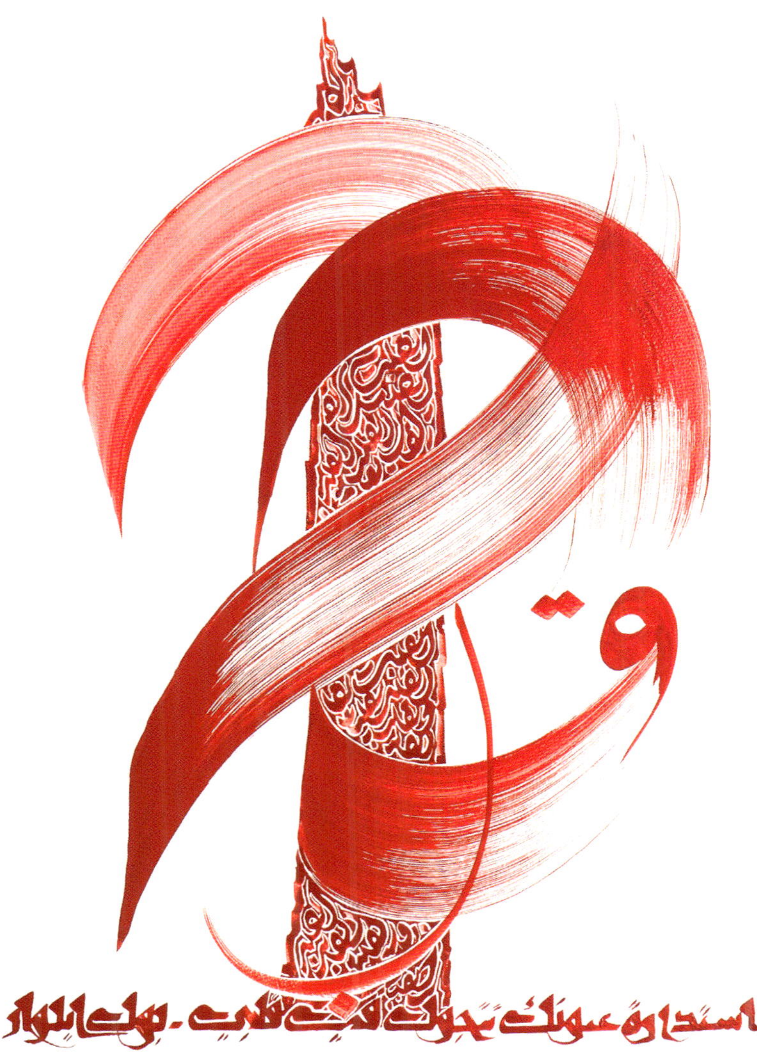

الحمد لله سبحانه تبارك وتعالى رب العالمين

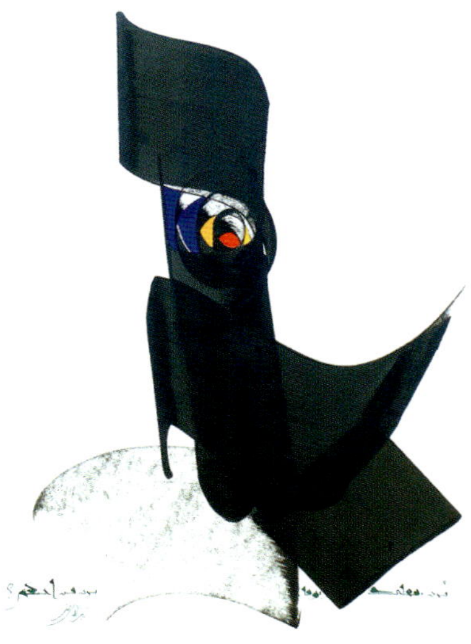

◀

One day, my eyes will see the eyes of
the one I love?

Ibn al-Farid (1181–1234)

تُرى مقلتي يوماً تَرى من أحبّهم؟
ابن الفارض

▶

Make me always more astounded
at the excess of my love for you.

Ibn al-Farid

زِدْني بفرطِ الحُبّ فيك تحَيّرا
وارْحَم حشـئً بلَظى هواكَ تسعّرا
ابن الفارض

The more I love you, the more bewildered I grow.
Have mercy on a heart blazing brightly with love.
If I ask to see you in reality,
Allow me, let not your answer be no –
O heart, you promised me patience
In loving them, so beware boredom.
Passion is life, so die for it
Willingly: you may die and be forgiven.

Ibn al-Farid

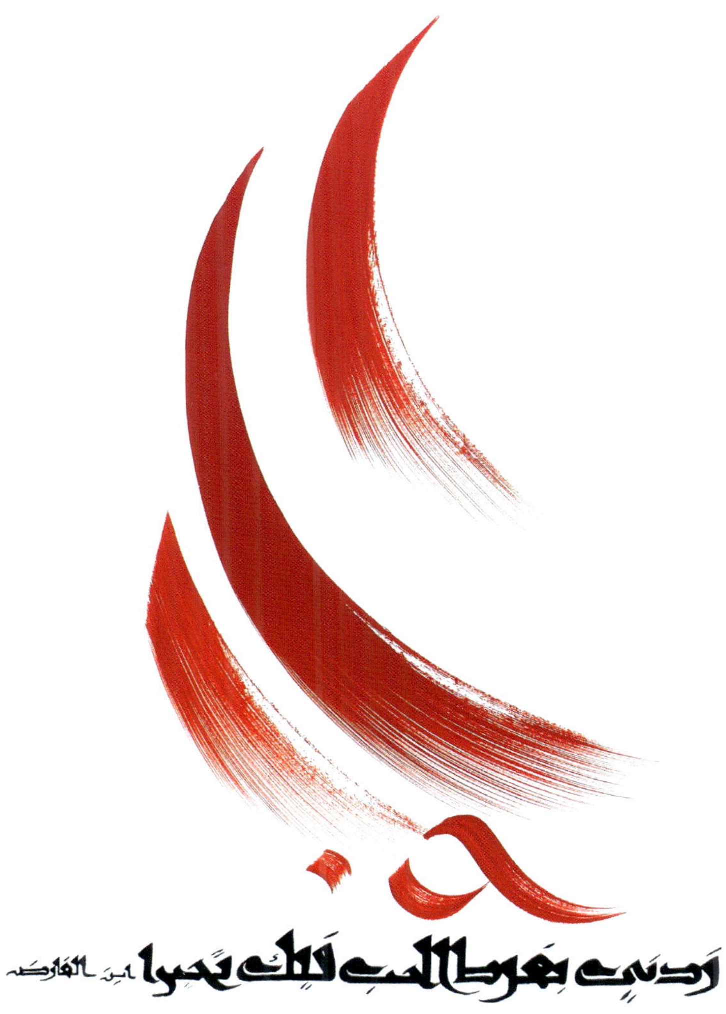

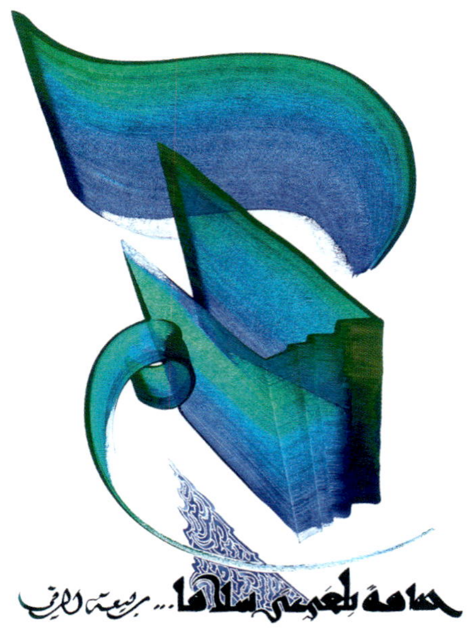

▲ ▶

Dove, give my best wishes of Peace.

Rabia Al Ruqui (?–814)

حمامةٌ، بلّغي عنّي سلاما.

ربيعة الرقي

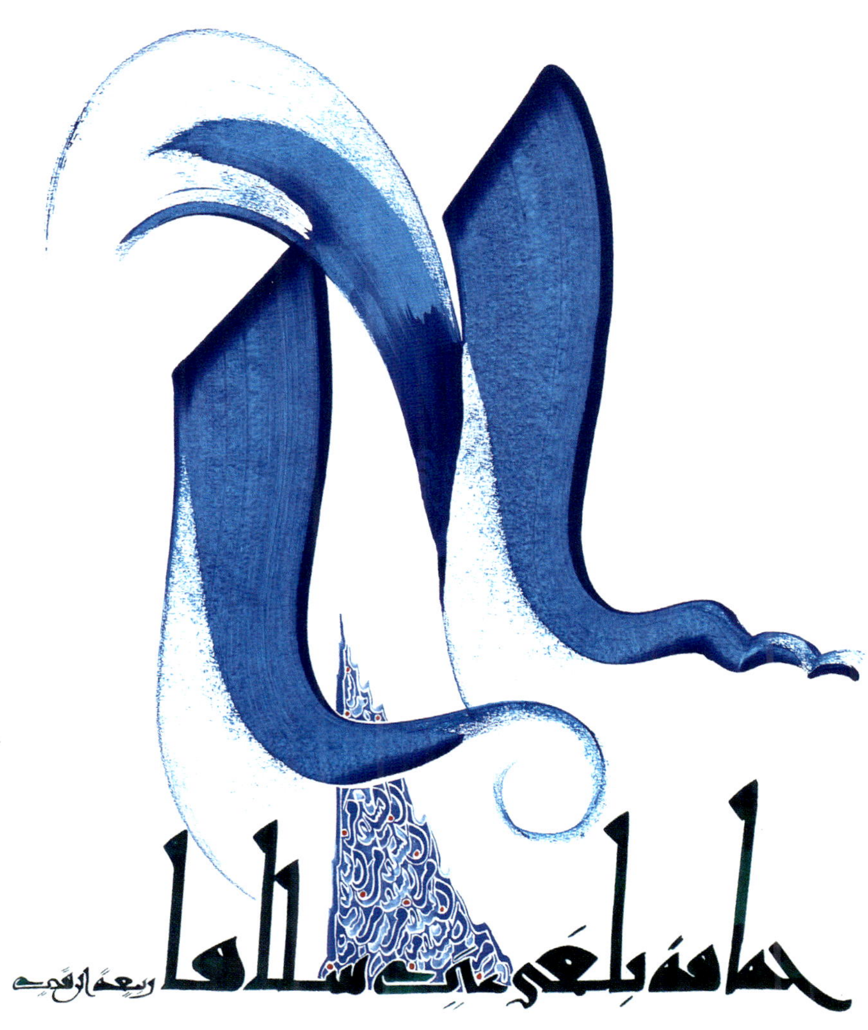

If your wave doesn't lift the sea
If your sails are subject to the winds
If your rudder does not break the swell
If your waves carry nothing but foam
If your cry is not louder than the ocean
How can you free the horizon?

Tahar Bekri (1951–)

اذا كان مَوْجُكَ لا يَهُزّ البِحار
وكان شِراعُكَ عَبْدا لِلرّياح
إذا كانتْ دَفّةُ مَرْكَبِكَ لا تُكَسِّرُ صَخَبَ المِياه
و كانتْ سُيولُكَ لا تَحْمِلُ إلاّ الزّبَد
إذا لمْ يَكُنْ صُراخُكَ أقْوى مِنَ المُحيط
كيف يُمْكِنكَ أنْ تُحَرِّرَ الأفُق؟

طاهر البكري

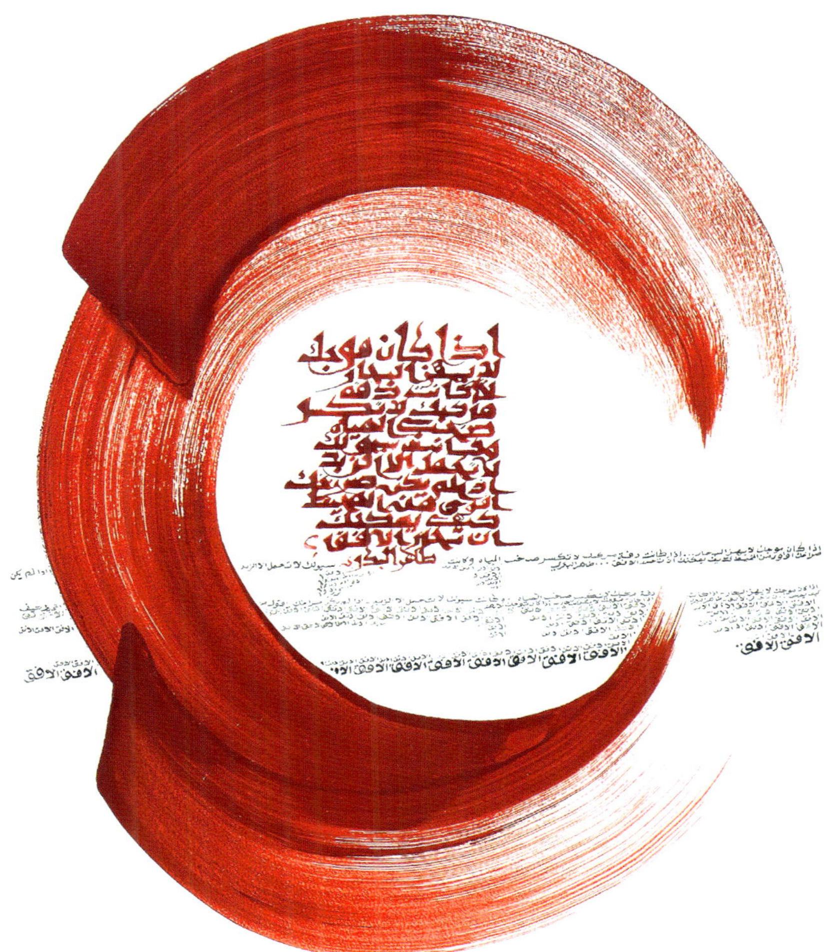

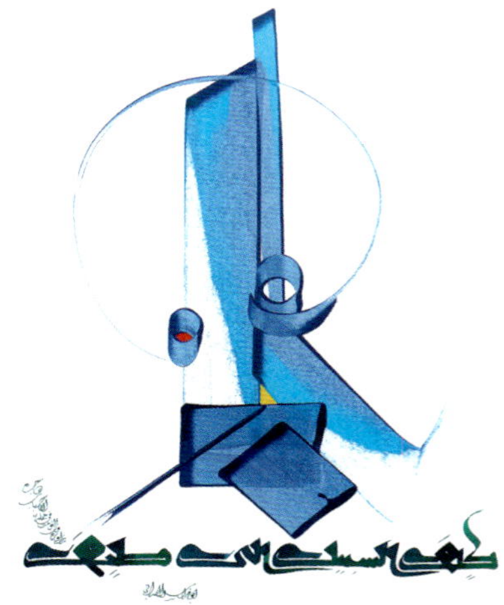

How to reach the dream that
visits him, when sleep, among
so many friends, leaves him?

Abu Firas al-Hamdani (932–968)

كيف السّبيل إلى طيفٍ يزاوره
والنّوم في جملة الأحباب هاجره
أبو فراس الحمداني

When a mourning dove cooed nearby, I said:
O neighbour, if you have sympathy for me
O neighbour, time has not been just to us.
Come, that I may share my worries with you, come.
Shall the prisoner laugh, while the liberated one cries?
Shall the sorrowful be silent, while the indifferent one weeps?
My eyes are more deserving of tears than yours,
Yet, in desperate times, my tears are rare.

Abu Firas al-Hamdani

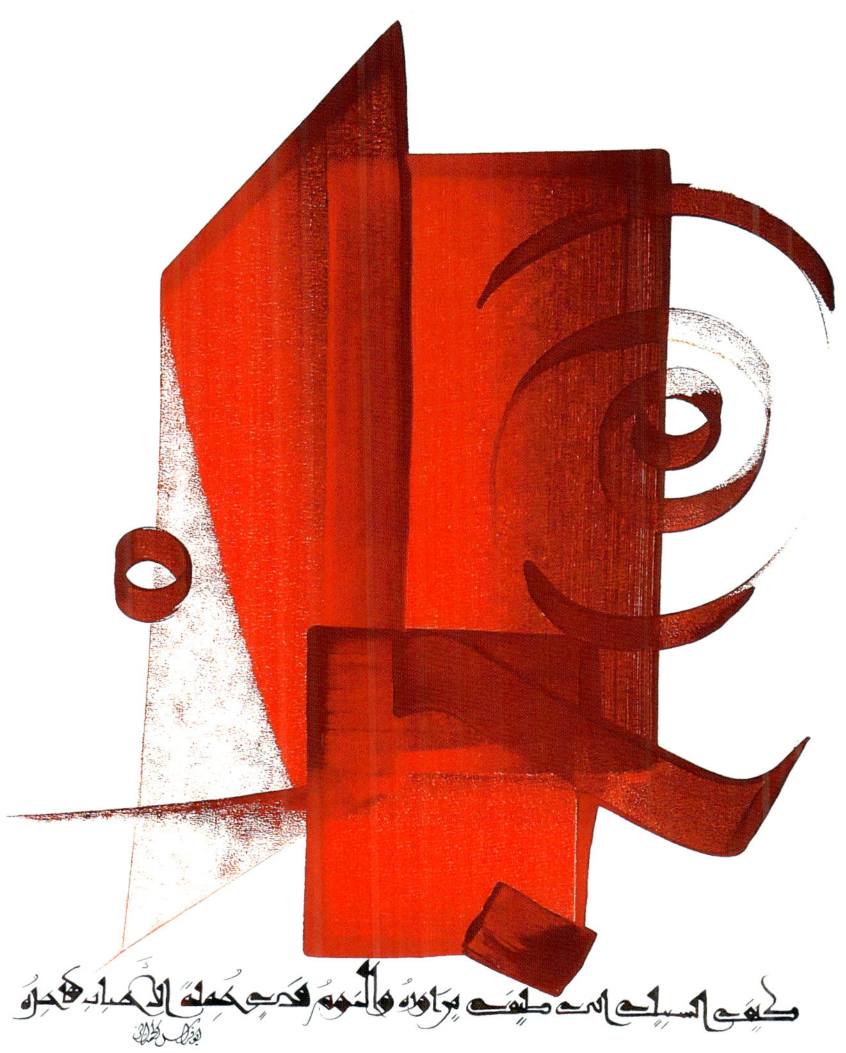

كفى بالسيف ناطقا وبليغا في الهيجا عن الحمد والذم
أبو تمام الطائي

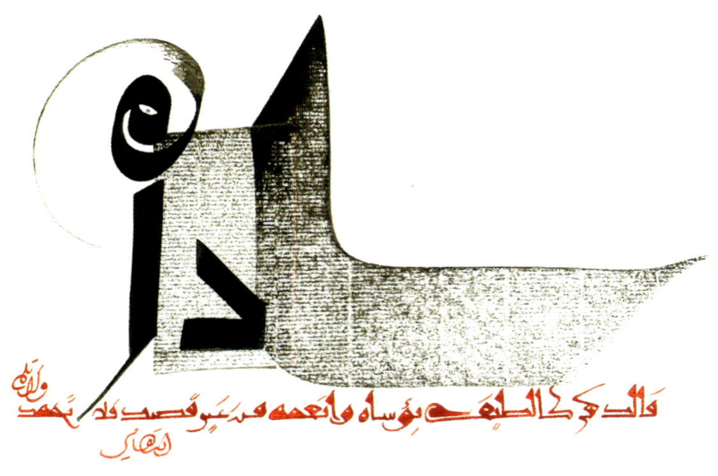

Time is like a dream, all its misfortunes
and its favours are unintentional.
Therefore, neither praise nor reproach.

al-Touhami (10th c.)

فالدّهر كالطَّيف بؤساه وأنعمه
من غير قصدٍ فلا تحمد ولا تلم
أبو الحسن التهامي

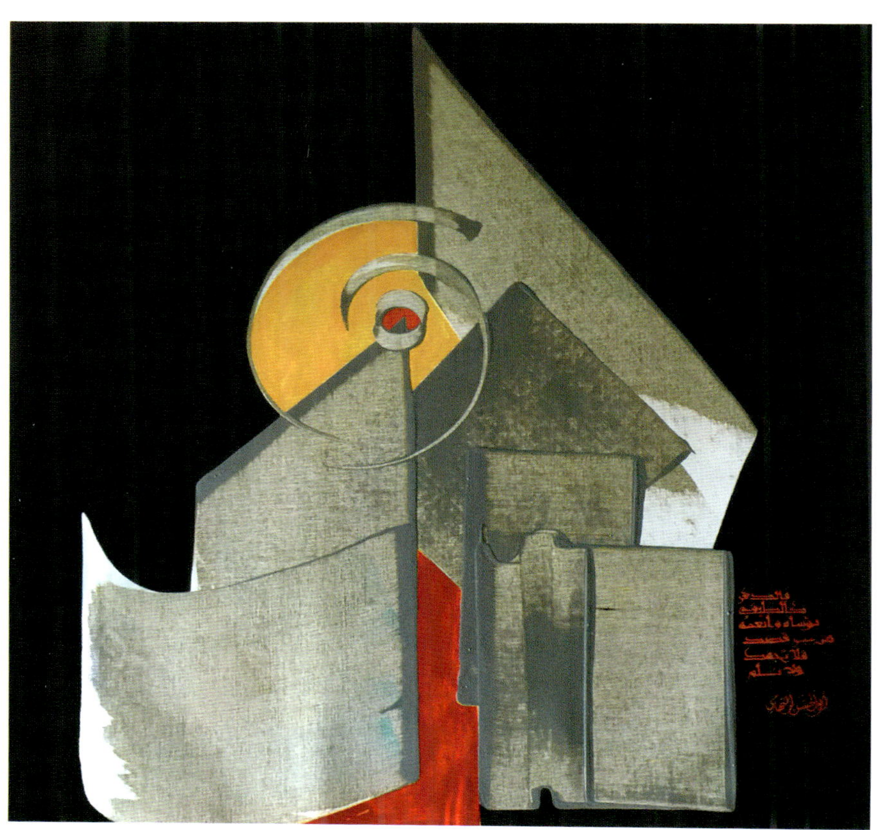

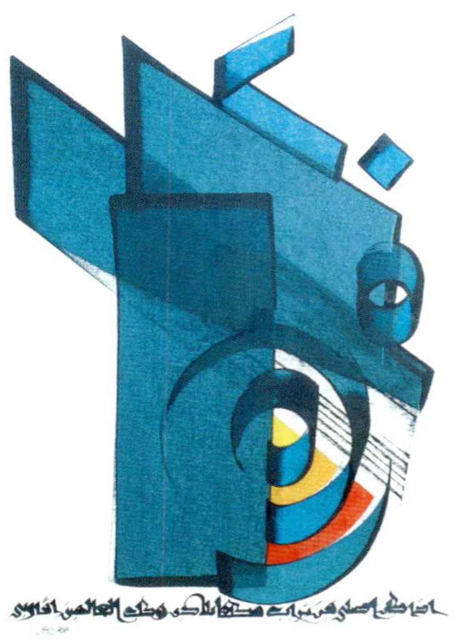

▲ ▶

If I am made of earth,
this latter is my country in its entirety,
and all of humanity are my brothers.

al-Siquilli (11th c.)

اذا كان أصلي من تراب فكلها
بلادي وكل العالمين اقاربي
أبو العرب الصقلي

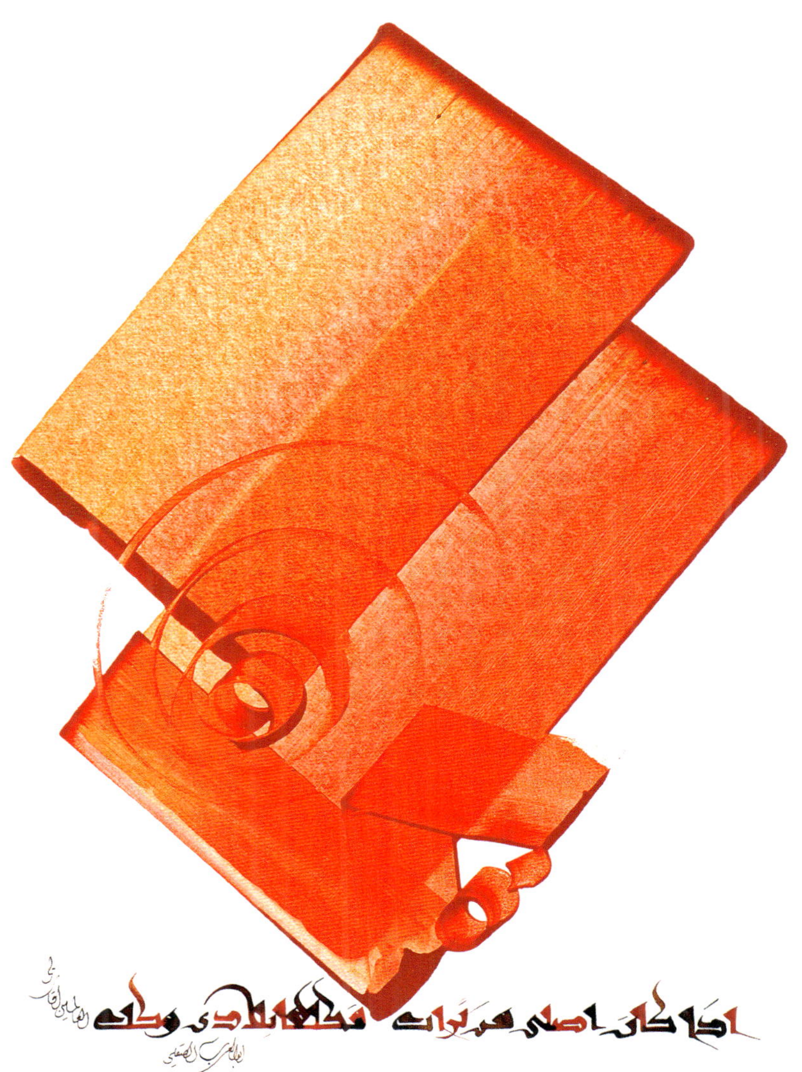

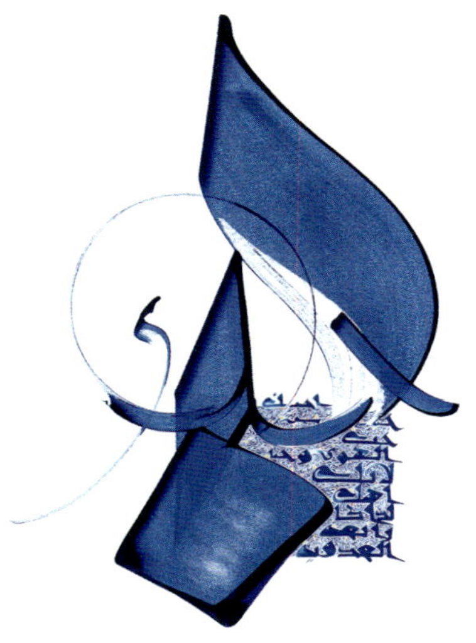

I love you with two kinds of love:
Passionate love, and the love you deserve.
In this passionate love,
I am consumed with you alone.

Rabi'a al-'Adawiyya (713–801)

أحبّك حُبّين: حبّ الهوى

وحبّاً لأنك أهلٌ لذاكا

فأمّا الذي هو حُبّ الهوى

فشُغلي بذكرِك عمّن سواكا

رابعة العدوية

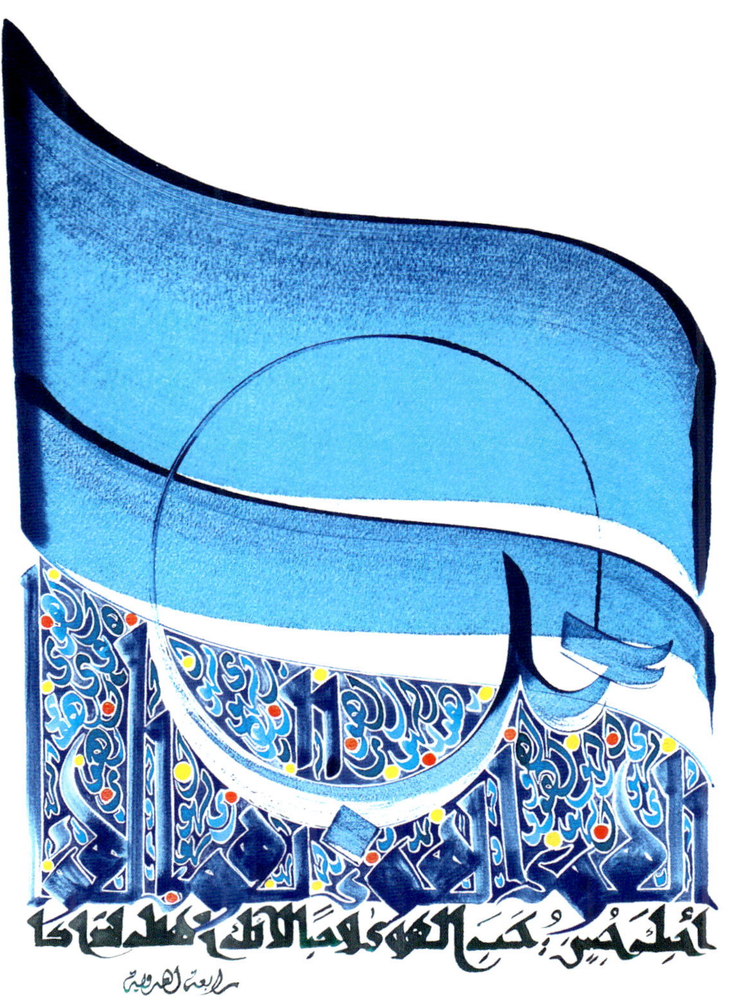

▶

I love the clouds ... the passing clouds ...
over there ... over there ... the wonderful
clouds!

Charles Baudelaire (1821–1867)

كم أحبّ الغيوم... تلك التي تمرّ... هناك
بعيداً... روائع الغيوم... هناك بعيداً.
بودلير

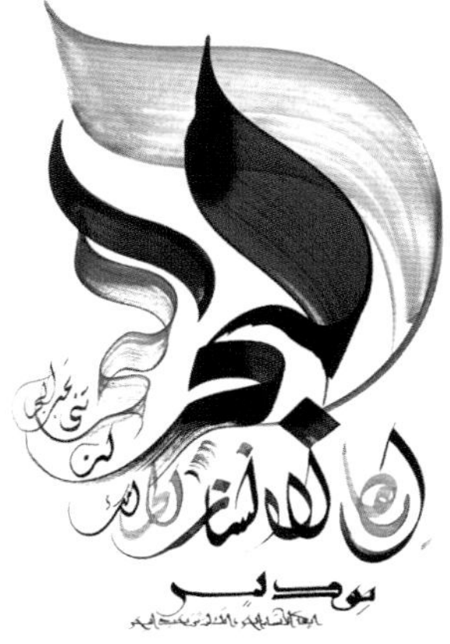

▲

Free man, you will always cherish the sea!
The sea is your mirror; you contemplate your soul
In the infinite unfurling of its waves,
And your spirit is no less bitter an abyss.

You delight in plunging into the bosom of your image;
You embrace it with your eyes and arms, and your heart
Is sometimes distracted from its own rumour
At the sound of this untamed and savage complaint.

Charles Baudelaire

أيّها الإنسان الحرّ، إنّك لن تني تحبّ البحر.
بودلير

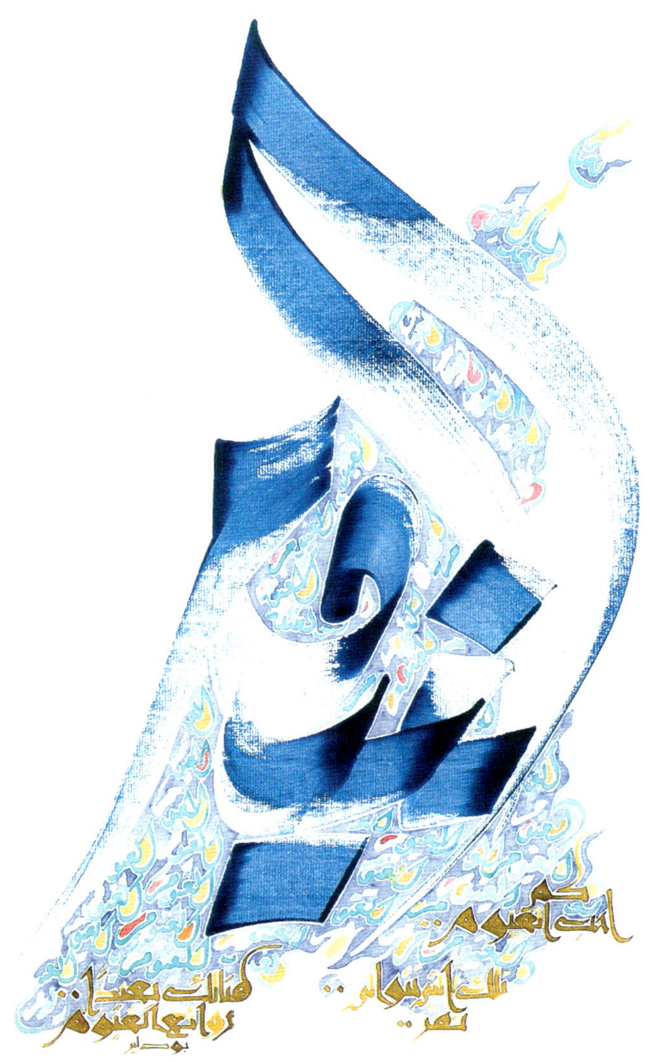

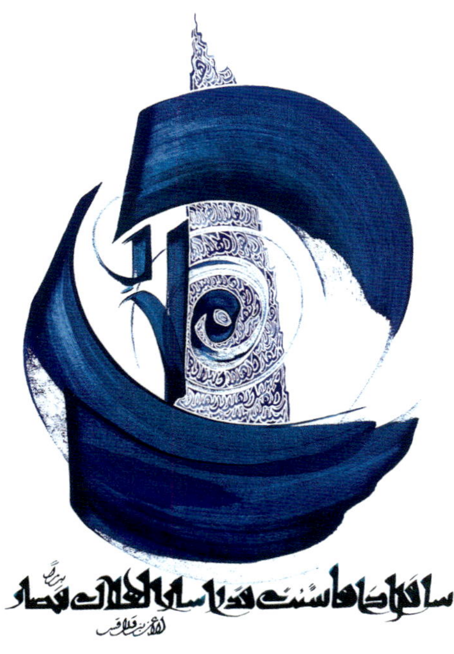

▲ ▶

Travel if you aim for certain value.
By travelling the skies the crescent becomes a
full moon.

Ibn Qalaqis (1137–1172)

سافر إذا ما شئتَ قدرا

سار الهلال فصار بدرا

الأعز بن قلاقس

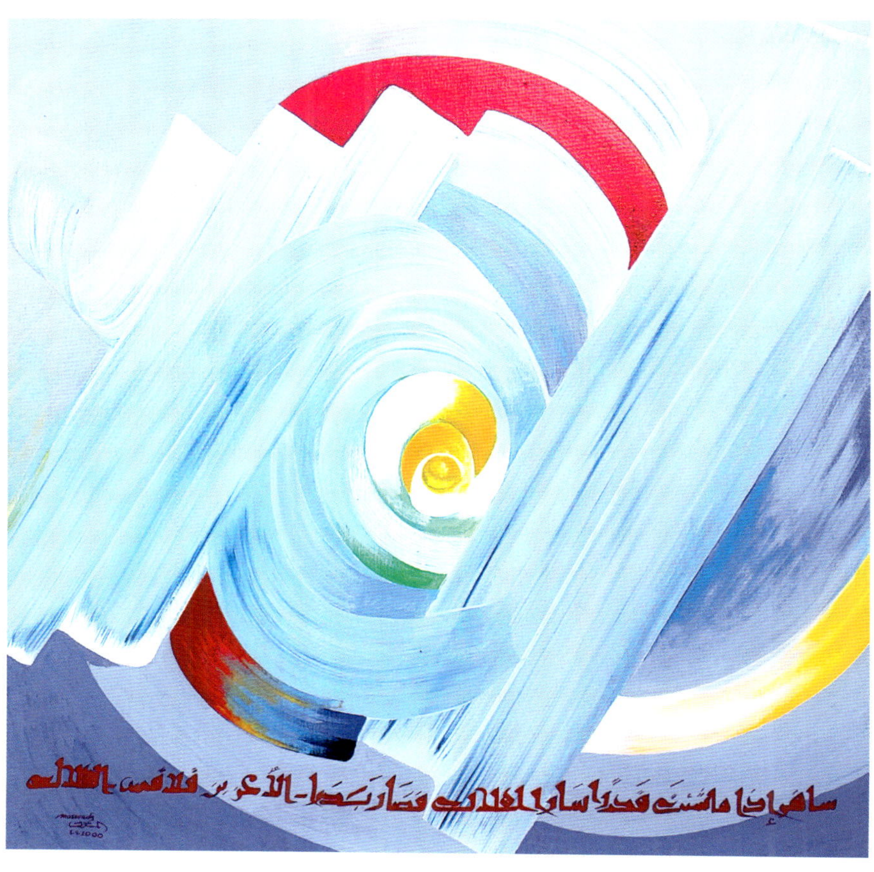
Massoudy
2000

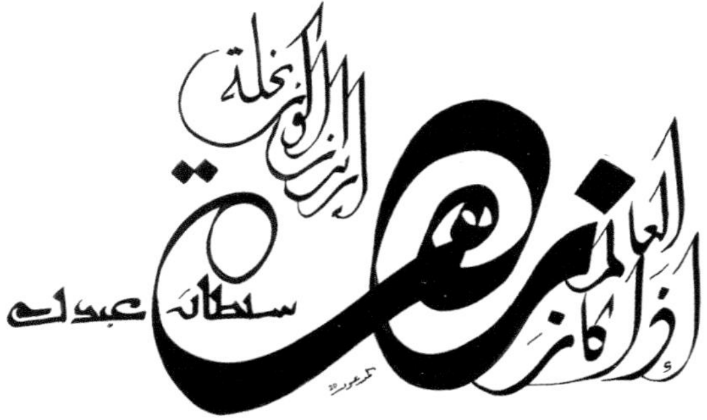

▲ ▶

If the world were a flower, I would like to be a bee.

Pir Sultan Abdal (1480–1550)

إذا كان العالم زهرة، أريد أن أكون نحلة.

سلطان عبدل

I am Pir Sultan Abdal, if I could be the mountains
If I could be the vines dotted with purple hyacinths
If I could be a bee in a world of flowers:
I could not find sweeter honey than the words of a friend.

Pir Sultan Abdal

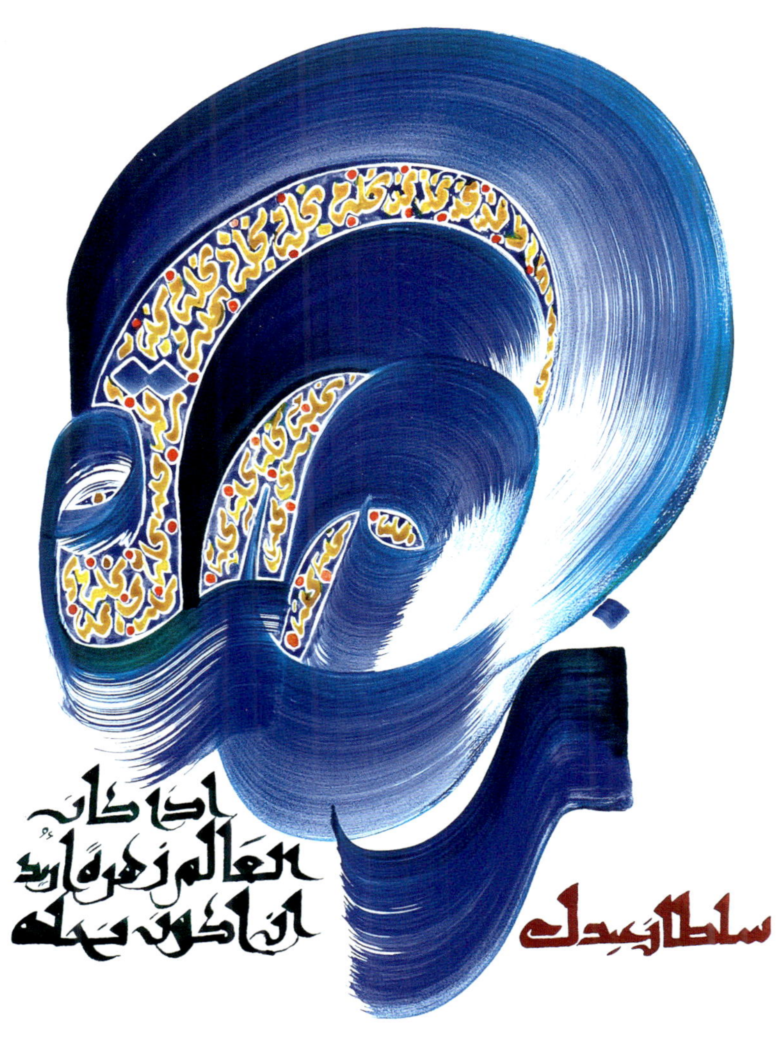

إذا كان العالم زهرة أريد أنا أكون نحلة
سلطان بن علي

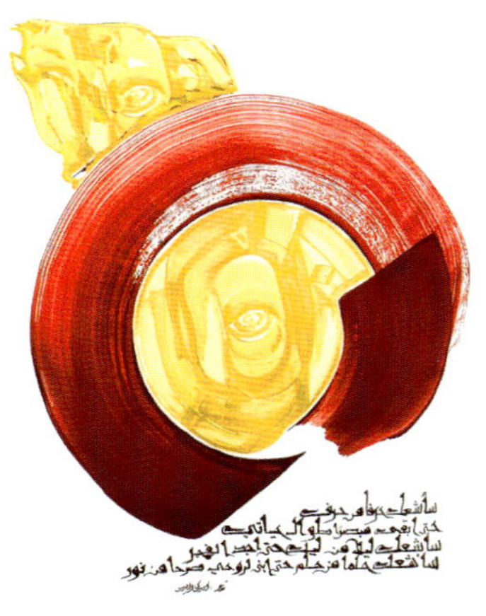

▲

With one letter, I will kindle the next,
And retain my sight all my life.
With one night, I will kindle the next,
Until I find the dawn.
With one dream, I will kindle a solution,
And build within my soul an edifice of light.

Adeeb Kamal Ad-Deen (1953–)

►

Life in exile has given me much sorrow,
But I turned it into a river of poetry.

Adeeb Kamal Ad-Deen

الغربة أعطتني الكثير من الأسى
لكنّني حوّلته إلى نهرِ شعر.
أديب كمال الدين

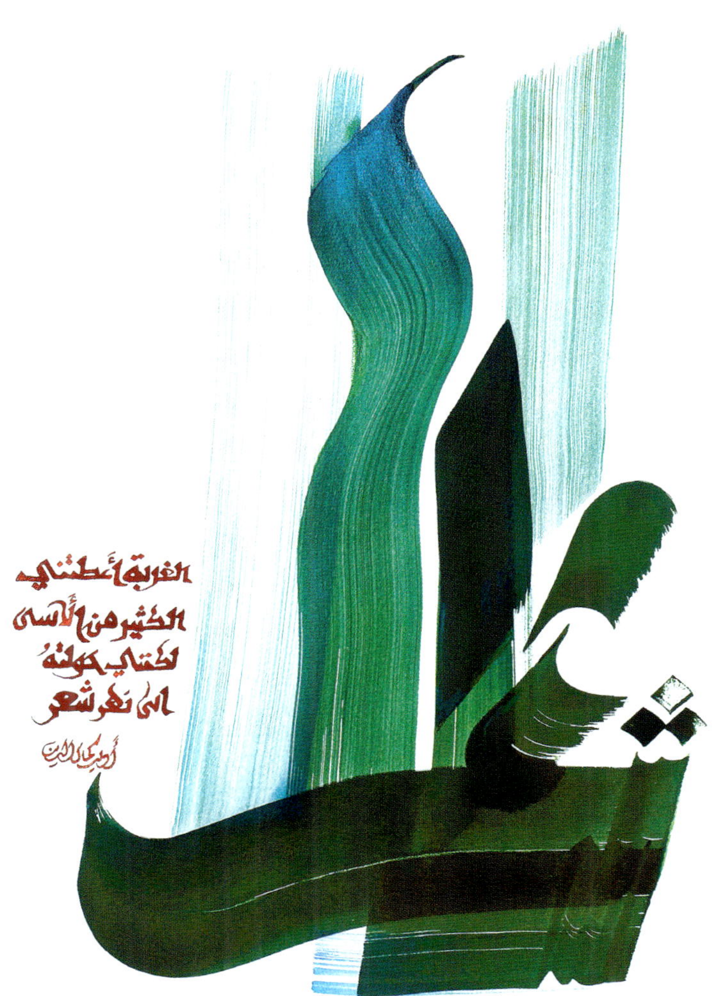

الغربة أعطتني
الكثير من الأسى
لكتابي حولته
الى نهر شعر
أمير كمال الدين

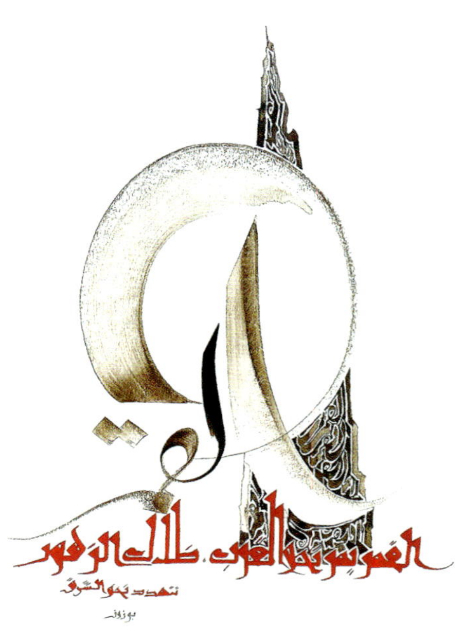

▲ ▶

The moon passes in the west
The shadow of flowers
Stretches to the east.

Yosa Buson (1716–1783)

القمر يمرّ نحو الغرب،
ظلال الورد تتمدّد نحو الشرق.
بوزون

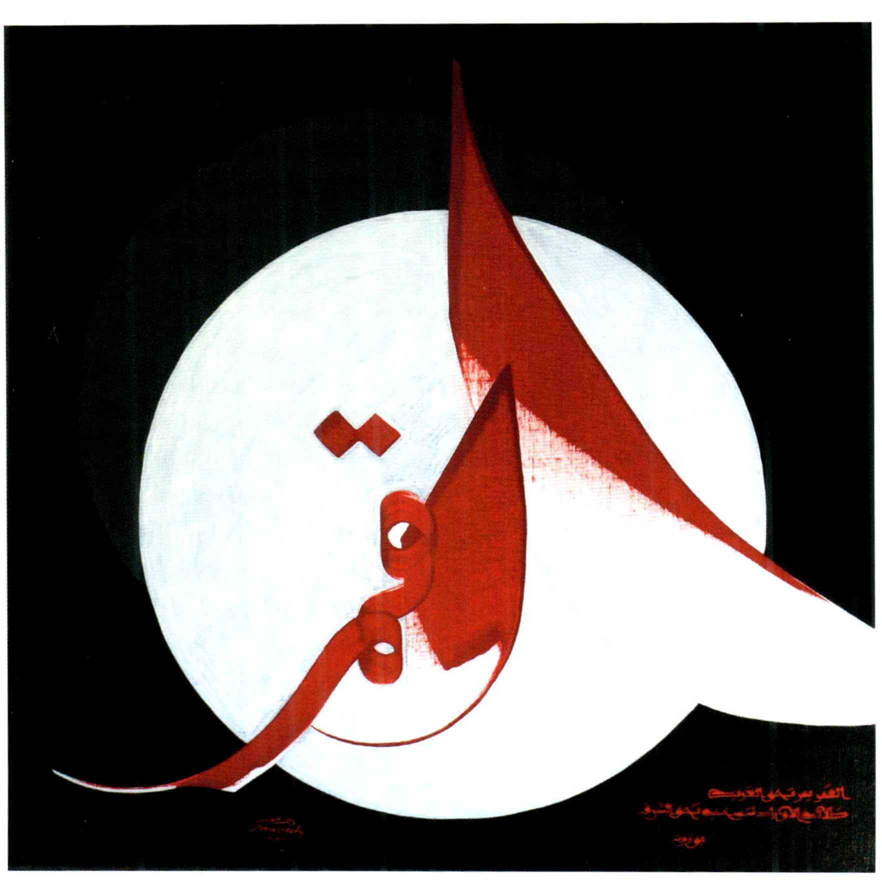

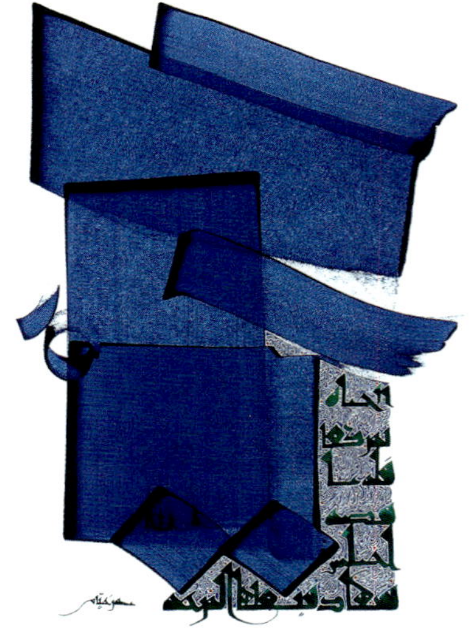

◀ ▶

Life passes like a mysterious
caravan, steal from it its
moment of joy.

Omar Khayyam (1048–1131)

الحياة تمرّ، كقافلة غامضة، خذ
منها دقيقتها المرحة.
عمر الخيّام

The pleasant Nowruz breeze awakens the roses,
How it warms my heart to see a cheerful face in the meadow.
Do not dwell on whatever unpleasantries were said yesterday;
Rejoice, and be happy for what is beautiful today.

Omar Khayyam

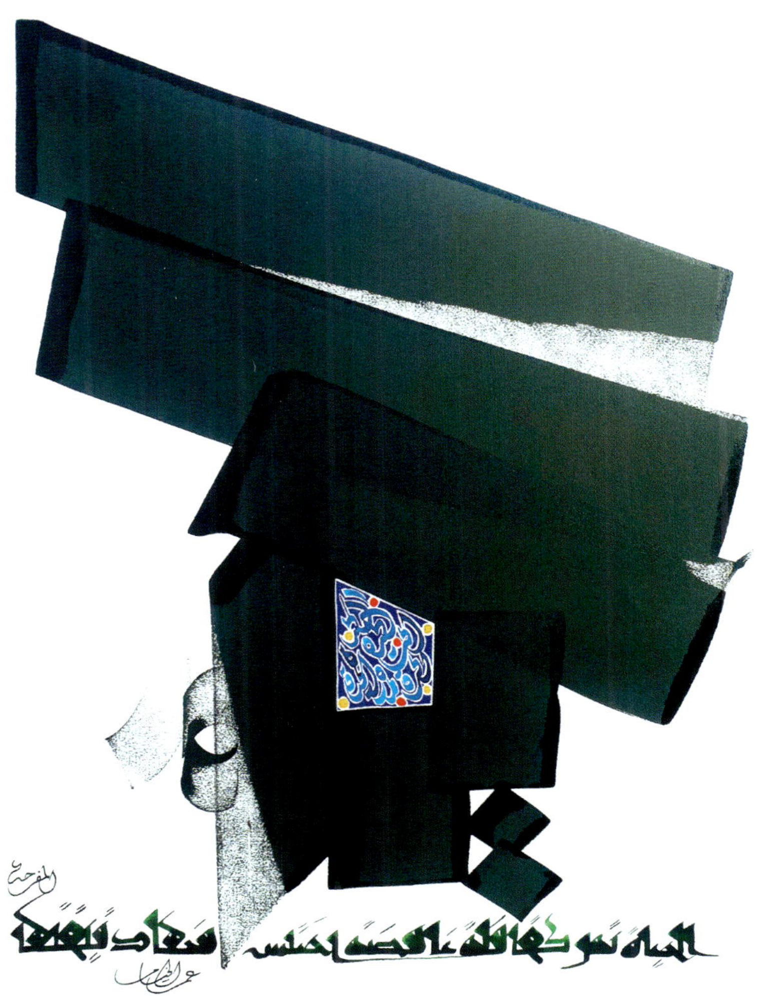

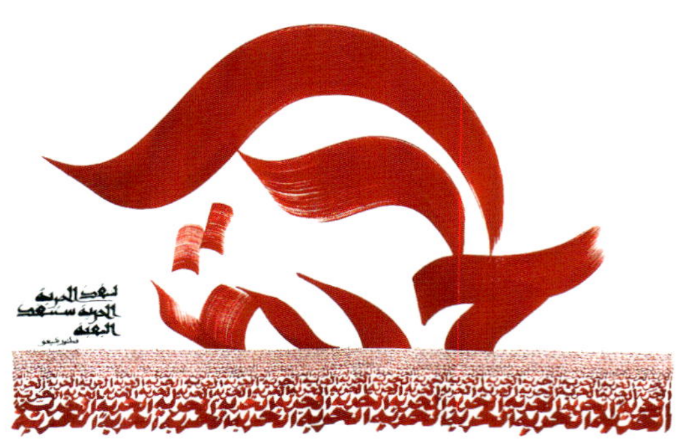

Save liberty, liberty saves the rest.

Victor Hugo (1802–1885)

لننقذ الحريّة، الحريّة تنقذ البقيّة.

فكتور هيغو

So long as ignorance and misery remain on Earth …

Victor Hugo

الجهل أكثر خطراً من البؤس.

فكتور هيغو

What right do you have to put birds in cages?
What right have you to take these singers from the hedgerows,
From the springs, the dawn, the clouds, the winds?
What right have you to rob the living of their life?
Man, do you think that God, this father, gives birth to
The wing to hang on your window nail?
Can't you live happily and contentedly without it?
What have all these innocent people done
To be in prison with their nest and their female?

Victor Hugo

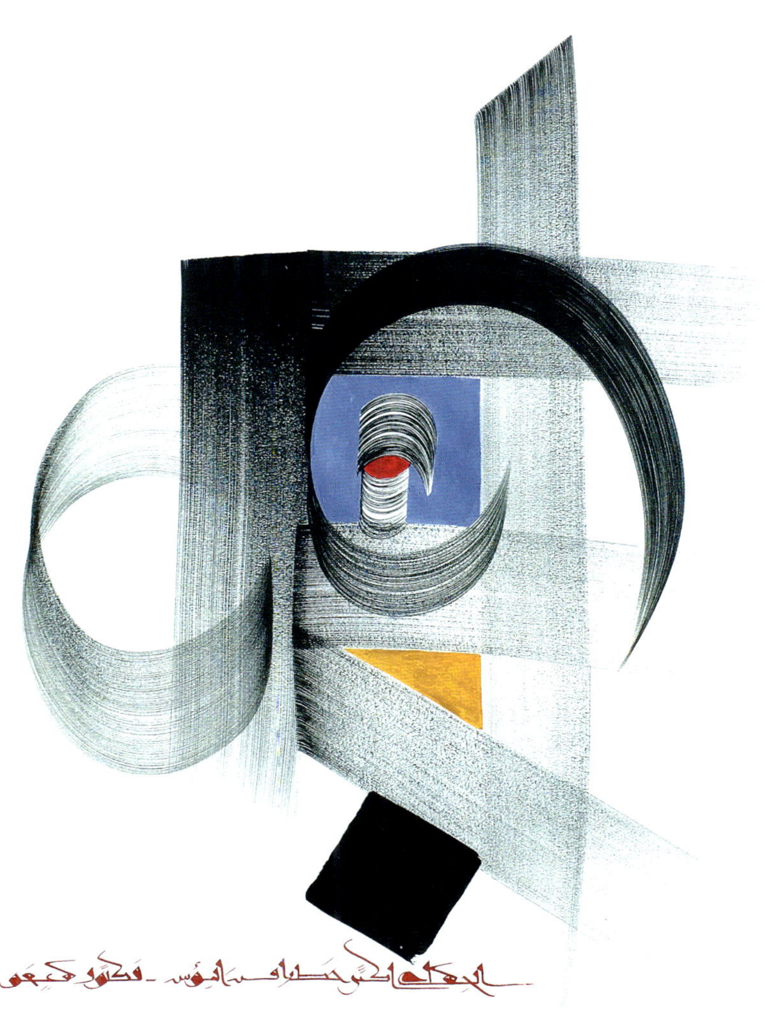

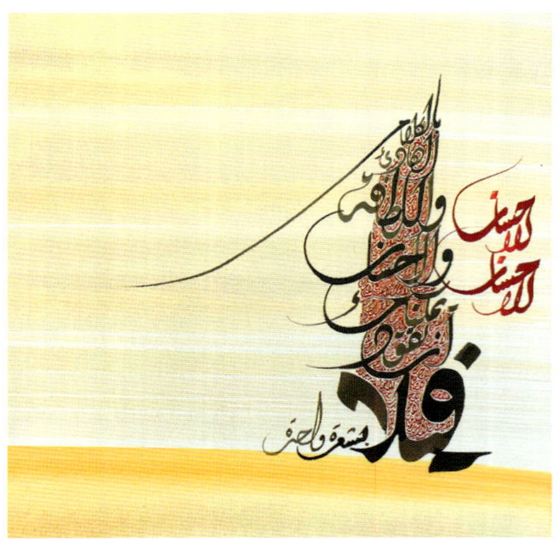

He who studies wisdom
but does not put it into
practice
is like a man who
ploughs a field but does
not sow it.

Saadi (1210–1292)

When conflict is imminent, use renunciation,
For understanding will close the door on conflict.
Be gentle in the face of quarrel and anger;
With gentle words, kindness and goodness,
You can drive an elephant with a hair.

Saadi

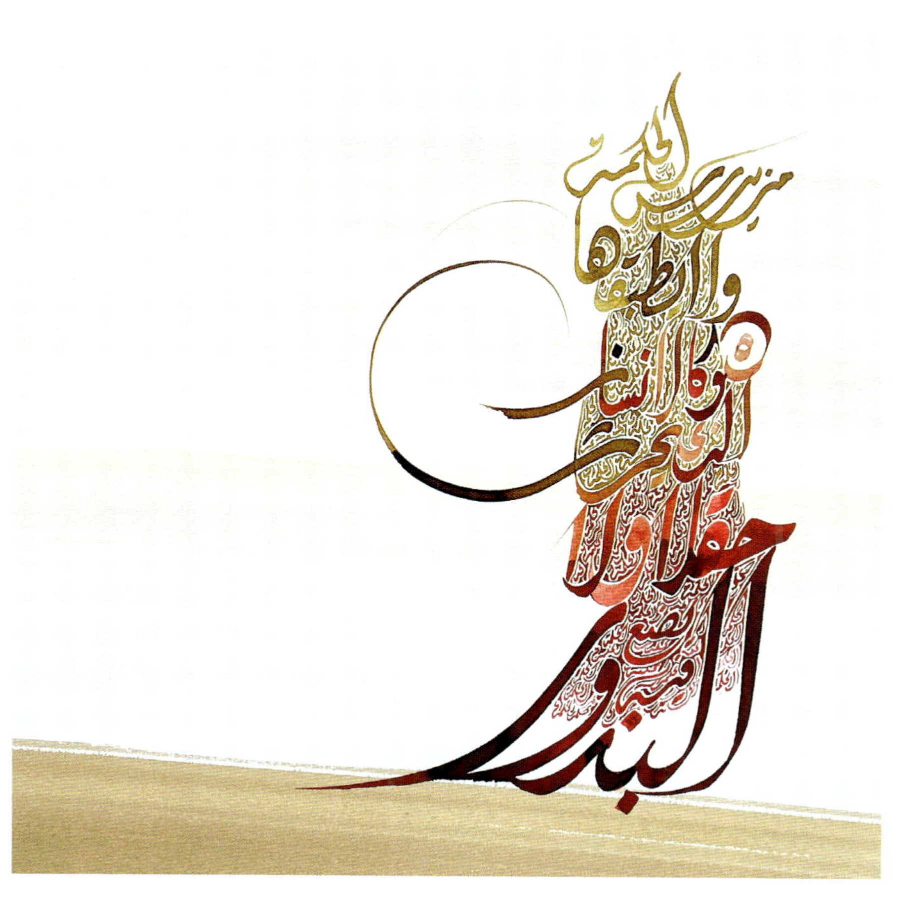

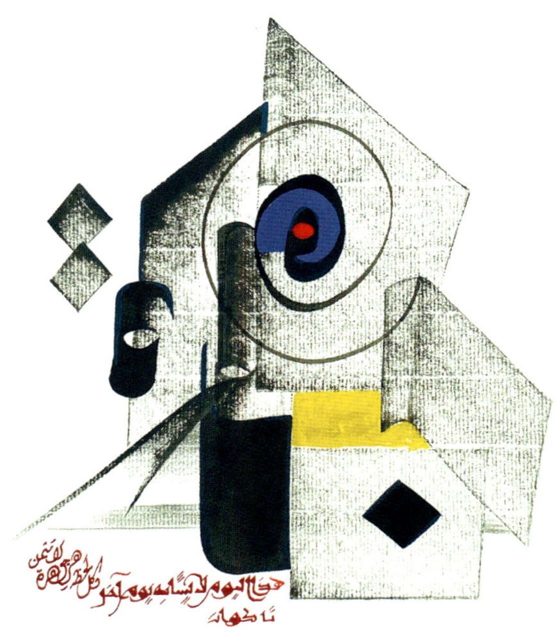

▲ ▶

This day will never be repeated again,
each instant is an inestimable jewel.

Takuan Soho (1573–1645)

هذا اليوم ليس له ما يشابهُه، وكلّ لحظة هي
جوهرة لا تثمَّن.

تاكوان سوهو

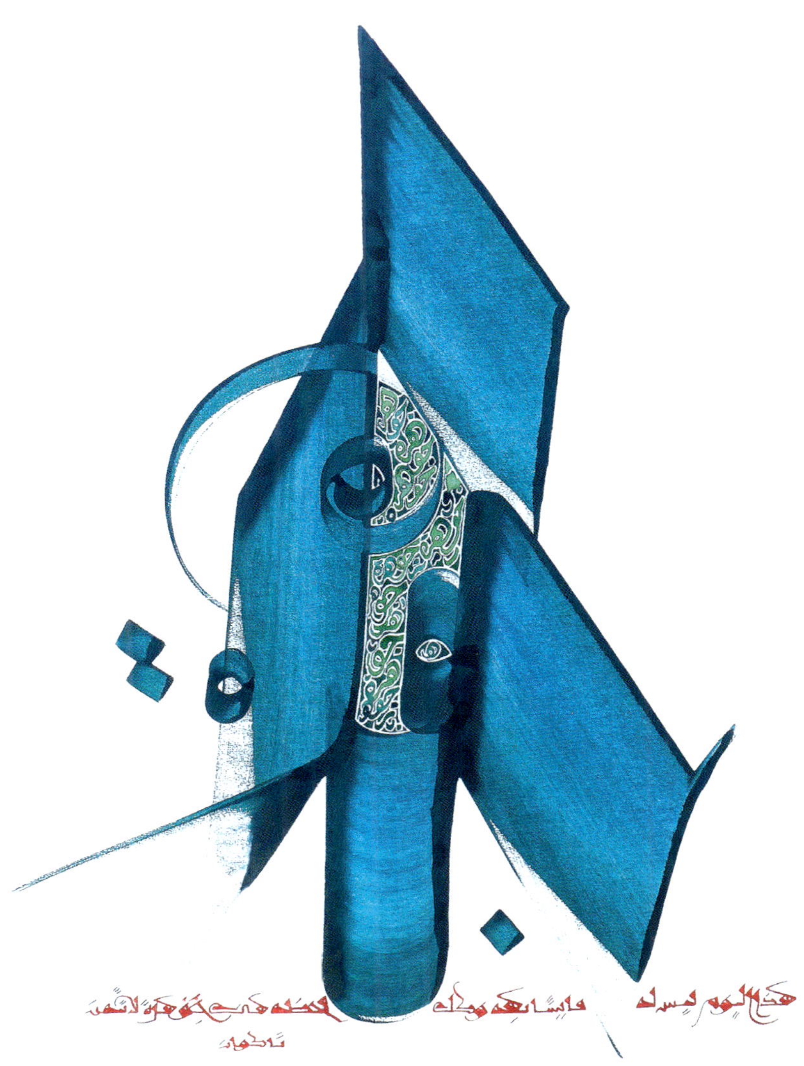

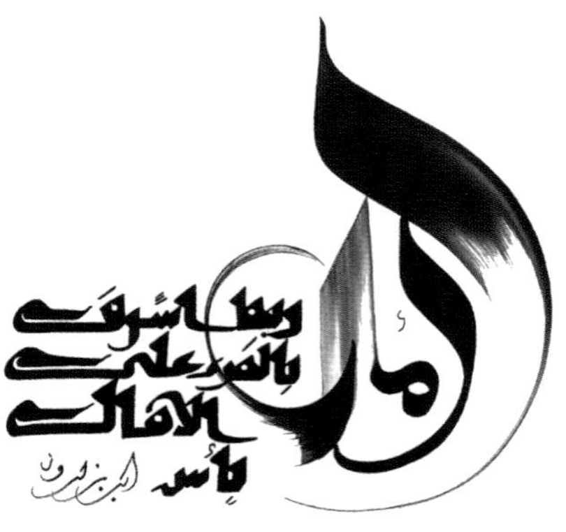

▲ ▶

Perhaps despair itself may lead us towards hope.

Ibn Zaydun (1003–1071)

ربما أشرف بالمرء

على الآمال يأس

ابن زيدون

Today my longing thoughts recall thee here;
The landscape glitters and the sky is clear,
So feebly breathes the gentle zephyr's gale,
In pity of my grief it seems to fail.
The silvery fountains laugh, as from a girl's
Fair throat a broken necklace sheds its pearls.
Oh, 'tis a day like those of our sweet prime,
When, stealing pleasures from indulgent Time
We played midst flowers of eye-bewitching hue,
That bent their heads beneath drops of dew.

Ibn Zaydun

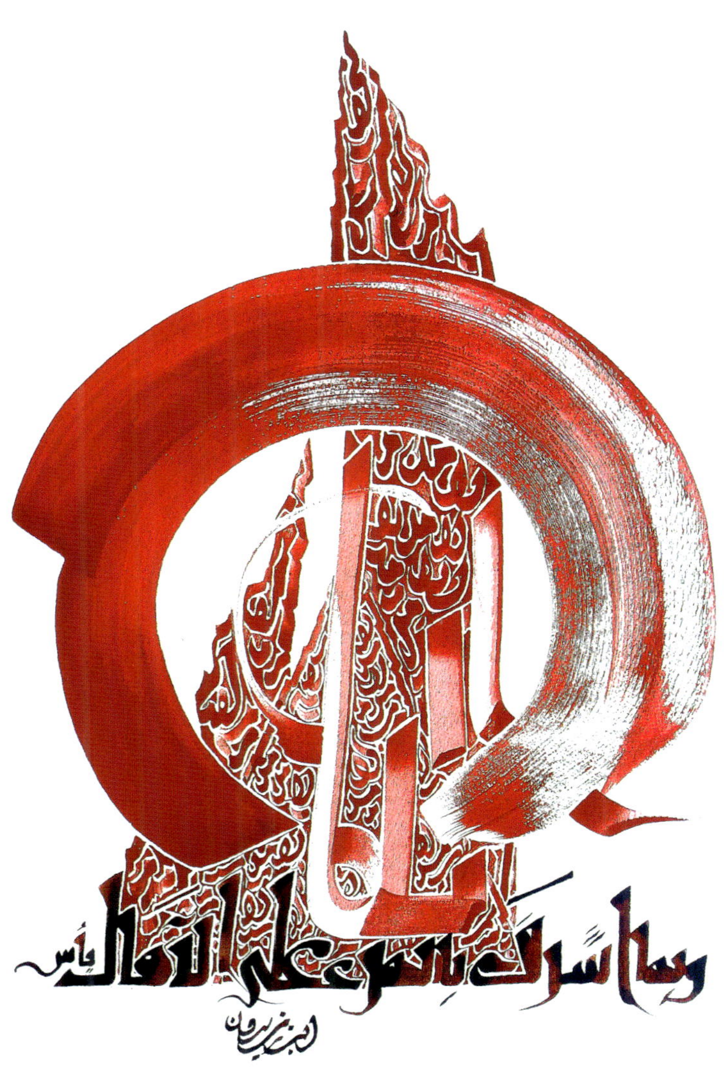

وسائل الإعلام وعلم النفس
ابن محمد بن رضوان

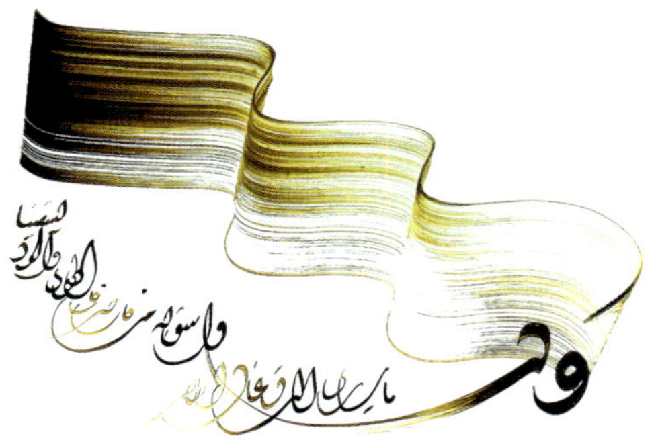

▲

Cloud, that brings lightning, go to the palace!
Shower with your blessings the one who with pure love
and tenderness showered me.

Ibn Zaydun (1003–1071)

يا ساريَ البرقِ غادِ القصرَ واسقِ به
من كان صِرفَ الهوى والودّ يَسقينا
ابن زيدون

▶

When you glanced at me I understood the meaning of love.

Ibn Zaydun

فهمْتُ معنى الهوى من وحي طرفكَ لي
ابن زيدون

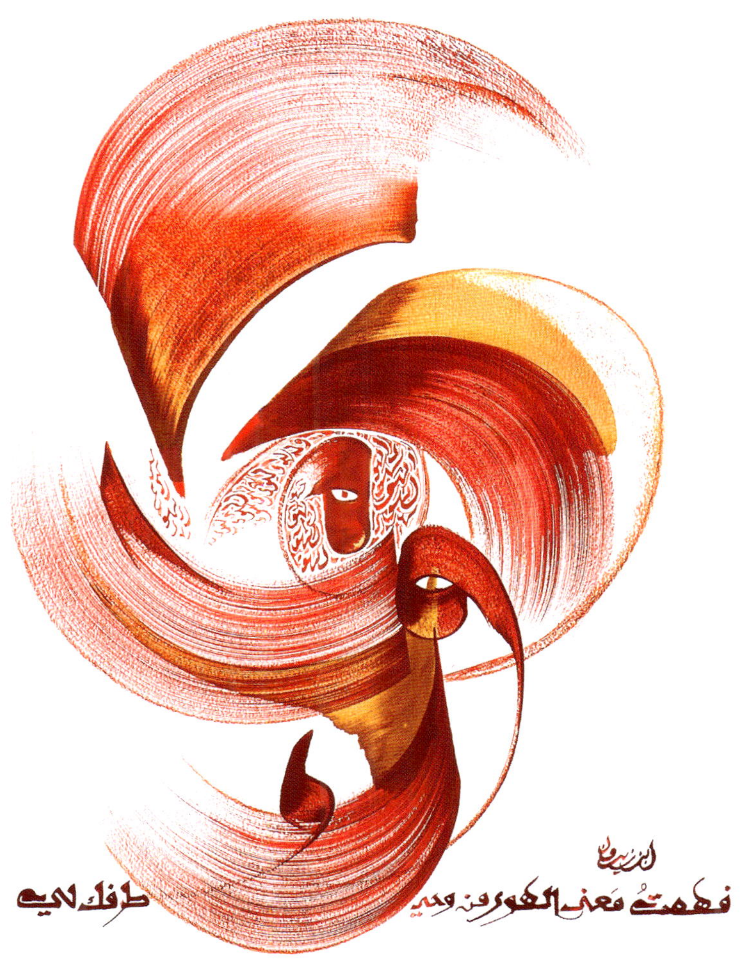
فهمتُ معنى الكون من وحي طرفك لي

▶

The heart flies, flies, flies, in the rays of spring.

Pierre Reverdy (1889–1960)

القلب يطير يطير يطير
في أشعّة الرّبيع.
بيار رفردي

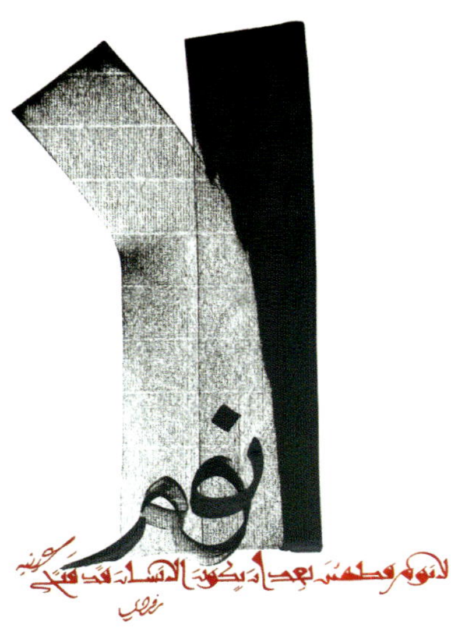

▲

We cannot rest easy when we have once opened our eyes.

Pierre Reverdy

لا نومَ مطمئناً بعد أن يفتح الإنسانُ عينيه.
بيار رفردي

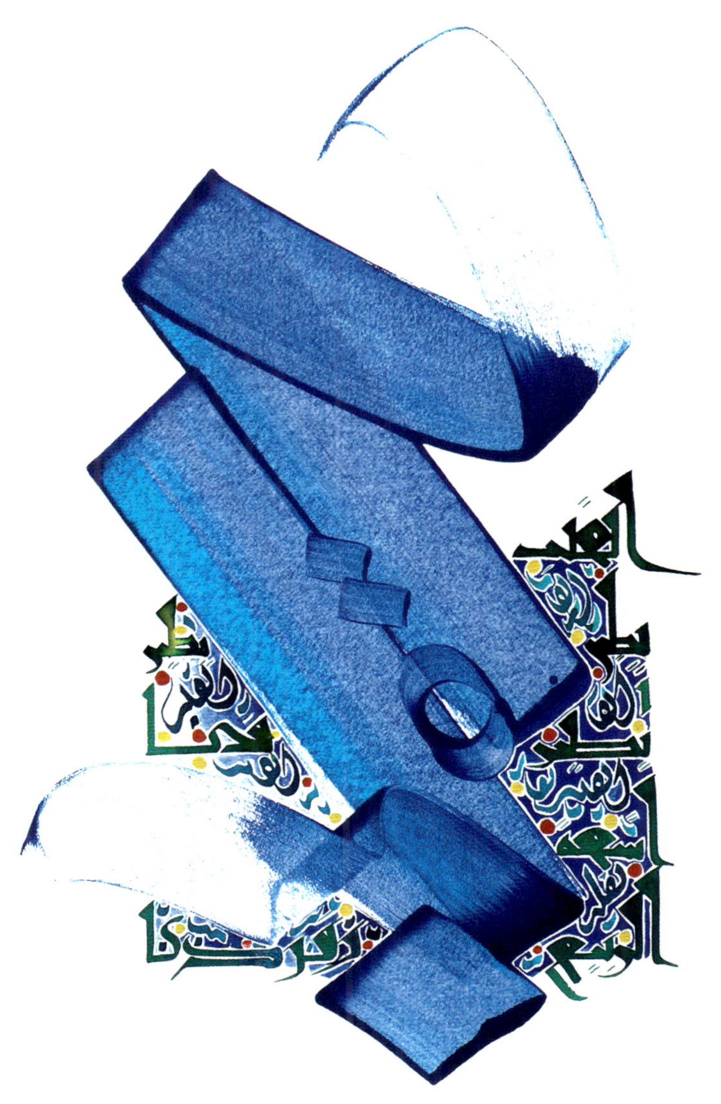

►

There are those who give with joy
and that joy is their reward.

Kahlil Gibran (1883–1931)

وبعضهم يعطي فرحاً وفرحته جزاؤه.
جبران خليل جبران

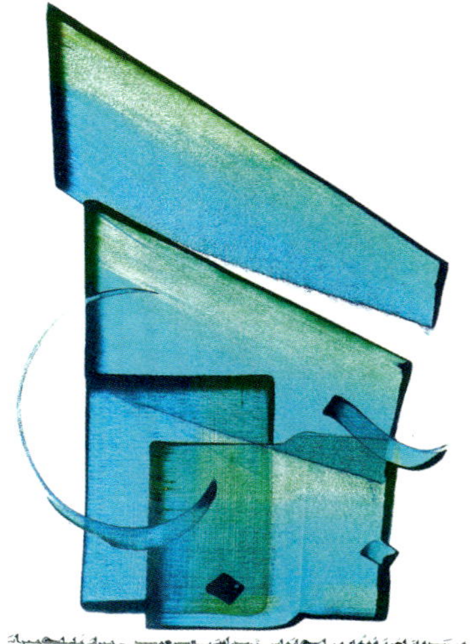

▲

Only when you drink from the river of silence,
Shall you indeed sing.
Only when you have reached the mountain top,
Then you shall begin to climb.
And when the earth shall claim your limbs,
Then shall you truly dance.

Kahlil Gibran

وعندما تبلغون قمّة الجبل، إنّما ستبدؤون بالصعود.
جبران خليل جبران

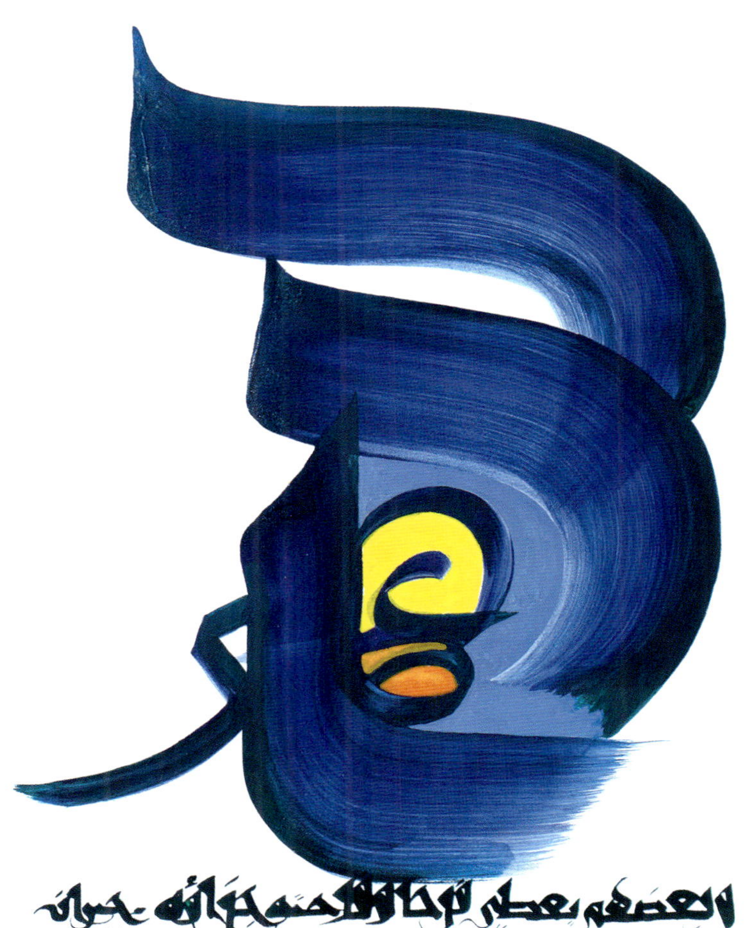

لا تعظهم بعطى لن كان الأحسن أنه بحسان

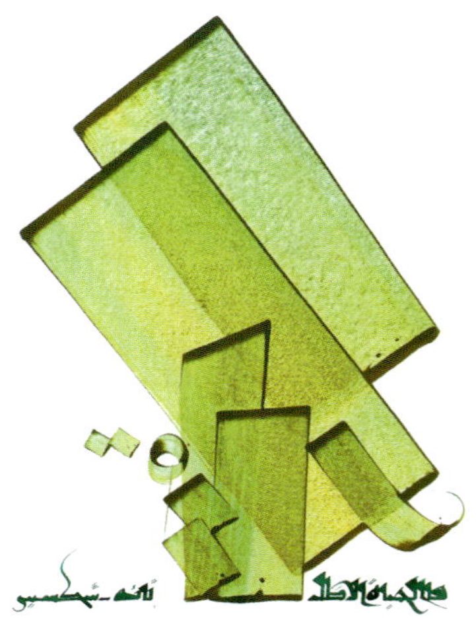

▲ ▶

She should have died hereafter;
There would have been a time for such a word –
Tomorrow, and tomorrow, and tomorrow,
Creeps in this petty pace from day to day,
To the last syllable of recorded time;
And all our yesterdays have lighted fools
The way to dusty death. Out, out, brief candle!
Life's but a walking shadow; a poor player,
That struts and frets his hour upon the stage,
And then is heard no more: it is a tale
Told by an idiot, full of sound and fury,
Signifying nothing.

William Shakespeare (1564–1616)

الحياة ما هي إلّا ظلّ تائه.

شكسبير

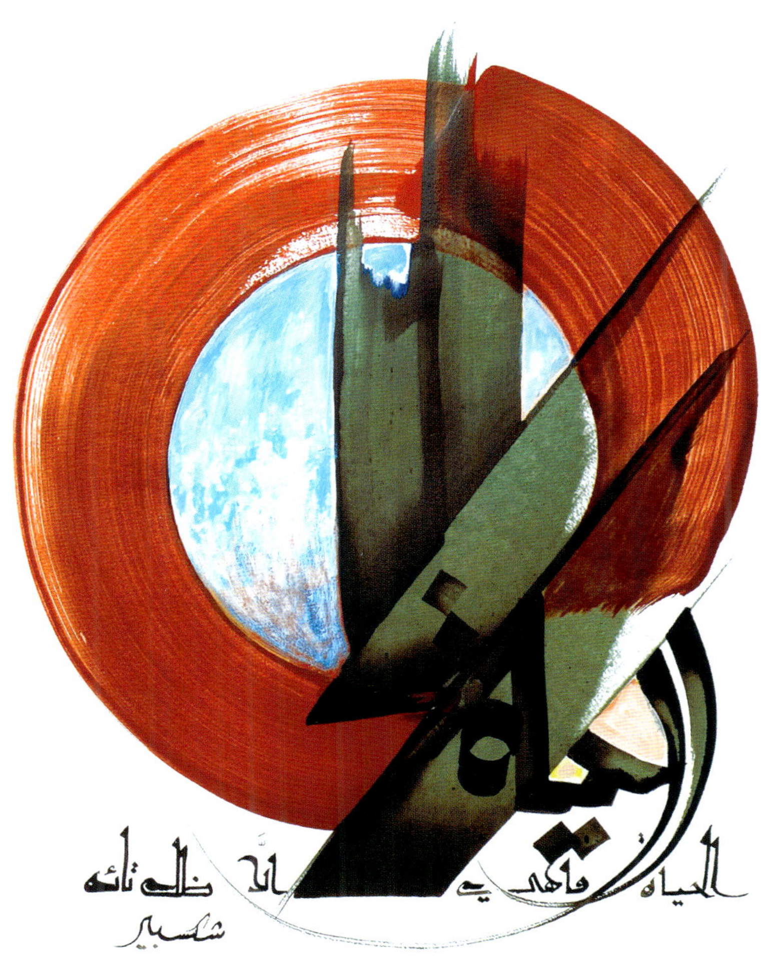

الحياة ماهي إلا ظل تائه
شكسبير

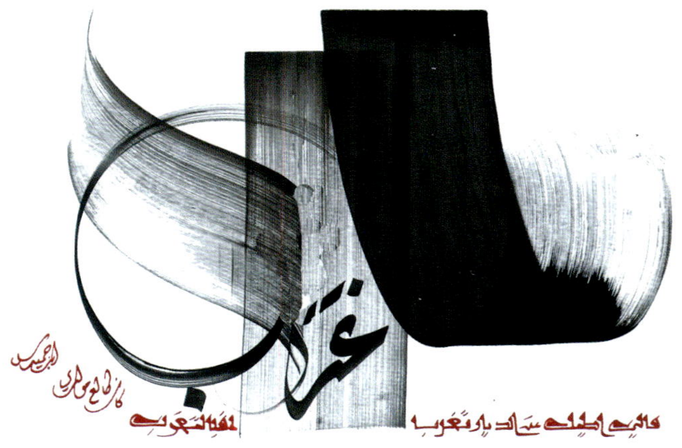

▲ ▶

What have I to prolong my absence from home?
Is exile the star of my birth?

Ibn Hamdis (1053–1133)

مالي اطيل عن الديارتغربا
أفبالتغرب كان طالع مولدي

ابن حمديس

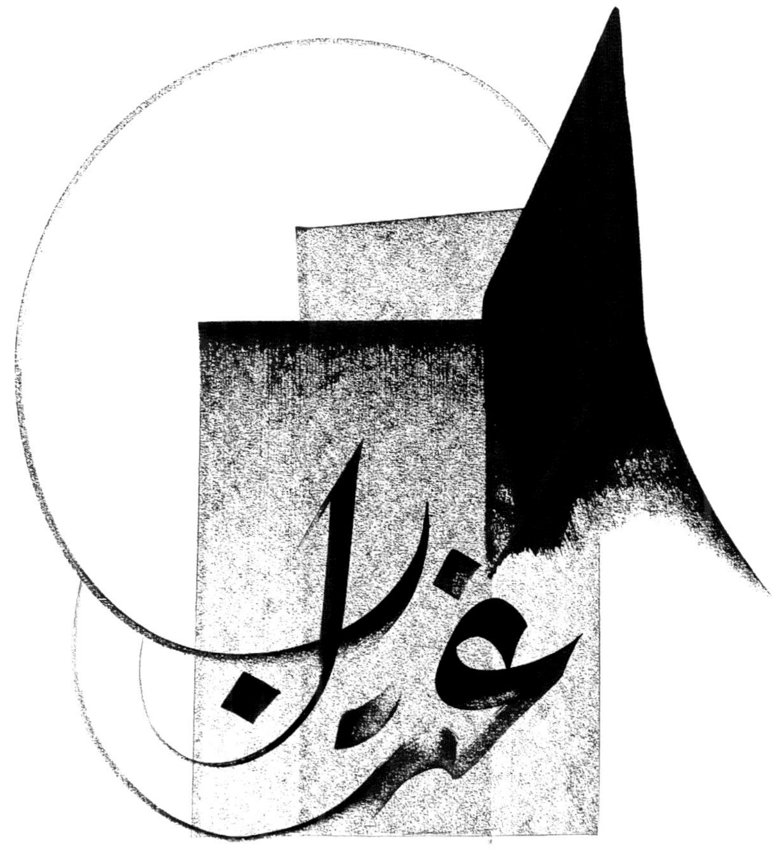

غزلان
ابن حمديس

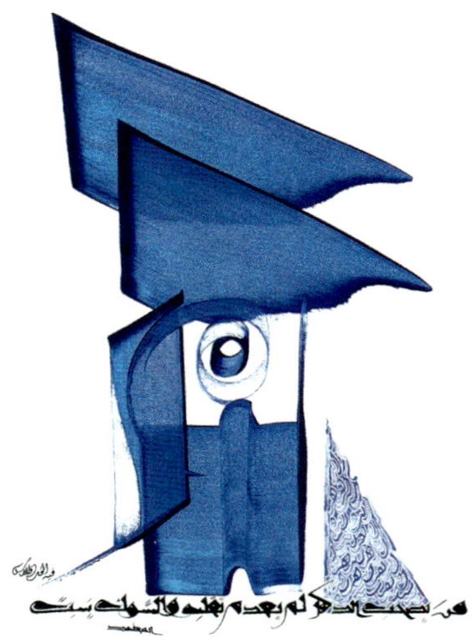

▲

He who devotes himself to time is not
spared from his jolts.
In thorns grow rose and myrtle.

al-Mu'tamid ibn Abbad (1040–1095)

من يصحب الدهر لم يعدم تقلبه
والشوك ينبت فيه الورد والآس.
المعتمد بن عباد

▶

Cursed be the time! What
precious little he offers, he
immediately tears!

al-Mu'tamid ibn Abbad

قبّح الدهر فماذا صنعا
كلما اعطى نفيسا نزعا.
المعتمد بن عبّاد

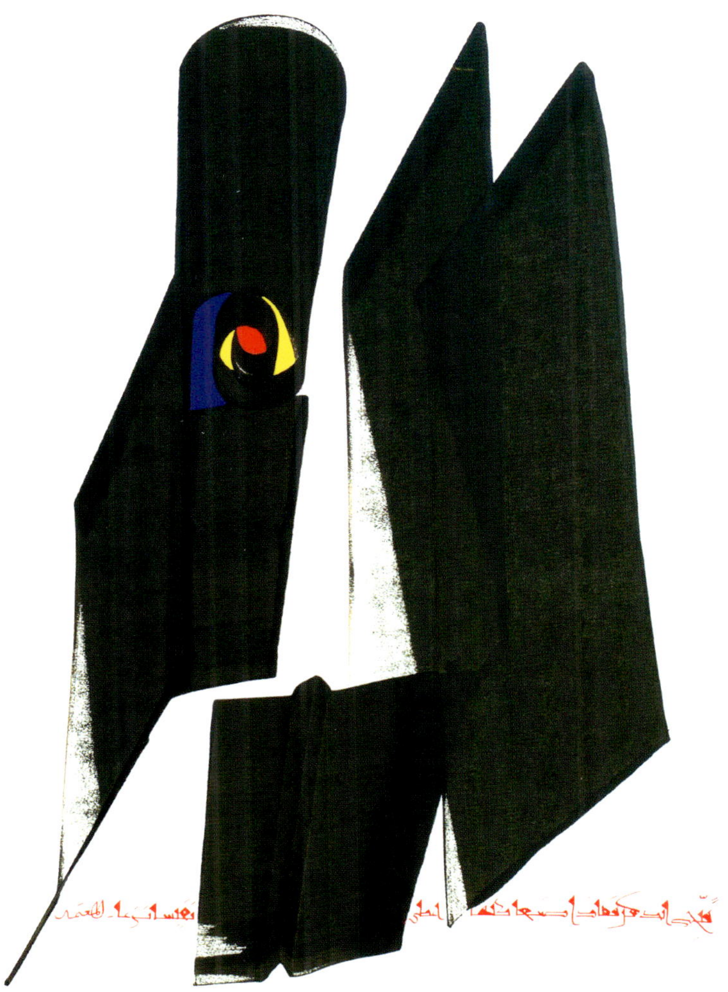

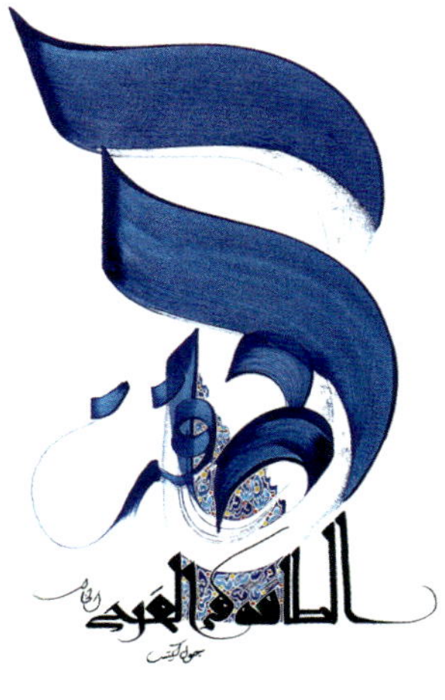

▶

I almost wish we were butterflies
and liv'd but three summer days.

John Keats (1795–1821)

أحلم أن نكون فراشاتٍ لا تملك زمناً
للعيش إلّا ثلاثة أيّام صيفية.
جون كيتس

▲

A thing of beauty is a joy for ever:
Its loveliness increases; it will never
Pass into nothingness; but still will keep
A bower quiet for us, and a sleep
Full of sweet dreams, and health, and quiet breathing.
Therefore, on every morrow, are we wreathing
A flowery band to bind us to the earth,
Spite of despondence, of the inhuman dearth
Of noble natures, of the gloomy days,
Of all the unhealthy and o'er-darkened ways
Made for our searching: yes, in spite of all,
Some shape of beauty moves away the pall
From our dark spirits.

John Keats

كلّ جمال هو فرح خالد.
جون كيتس

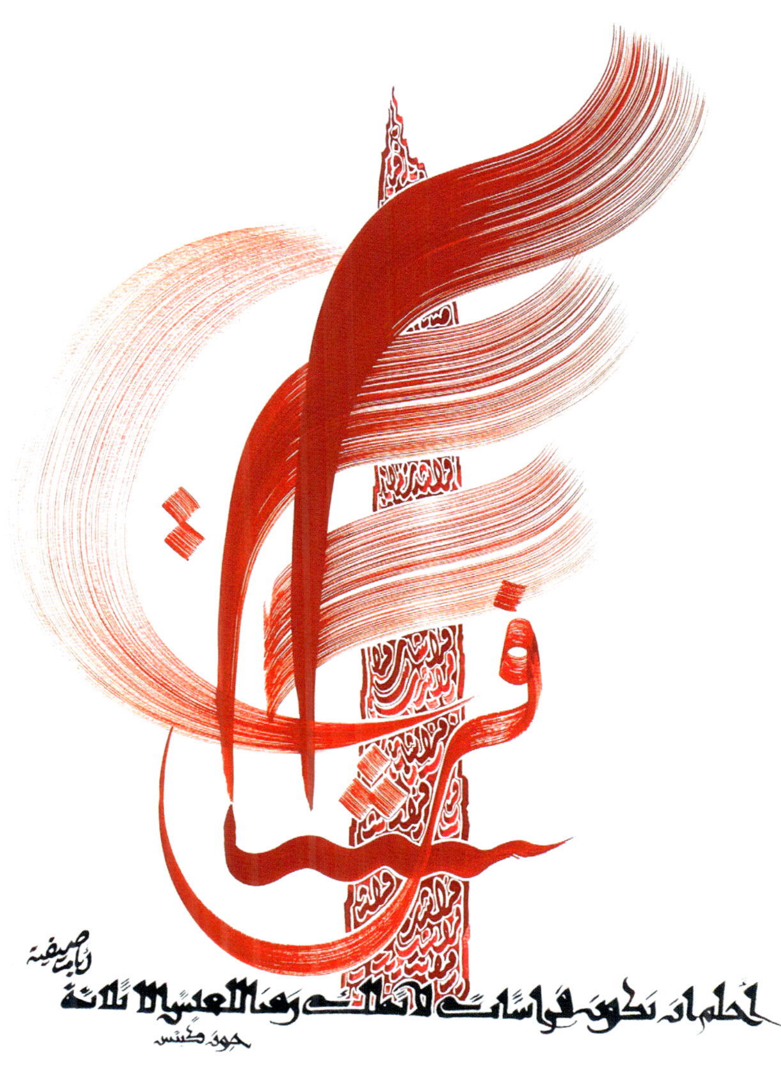

أيام صيفية
أحلم انه تكون لدي اساس لا أهلك وفي العيش ثلاثة
جون ديكنز

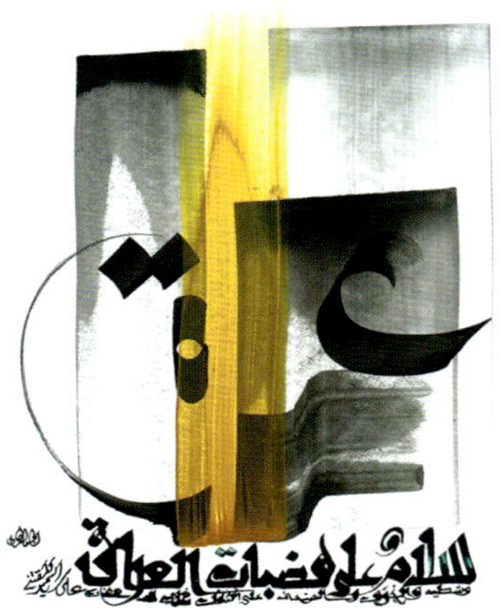

Hello to the hills of Iraq, to its two
rivers, to its friendly beaches.
Hello to the majestic palm tree lord.

Muhammad Mahdi al-Jawahiri
(1900–1997)

سلامٌ على هضبات العراق
وشطَّيهِ والجُرفِ والمُنحنى
على النّخل ذي السّعفاتِ الطِّوال
على سيّد الشّجر المُقتنى
الجواهري

Baghdad heart of Iraq,
Its memory and conscience,
May no wind ever trouble you.

Muhammad Mahdi al-Jawahiri

بغداد يا قلبَ العراق
ووعيَه وضميرَه،
لا زعزعتكِ رياحُ.
الجواهري

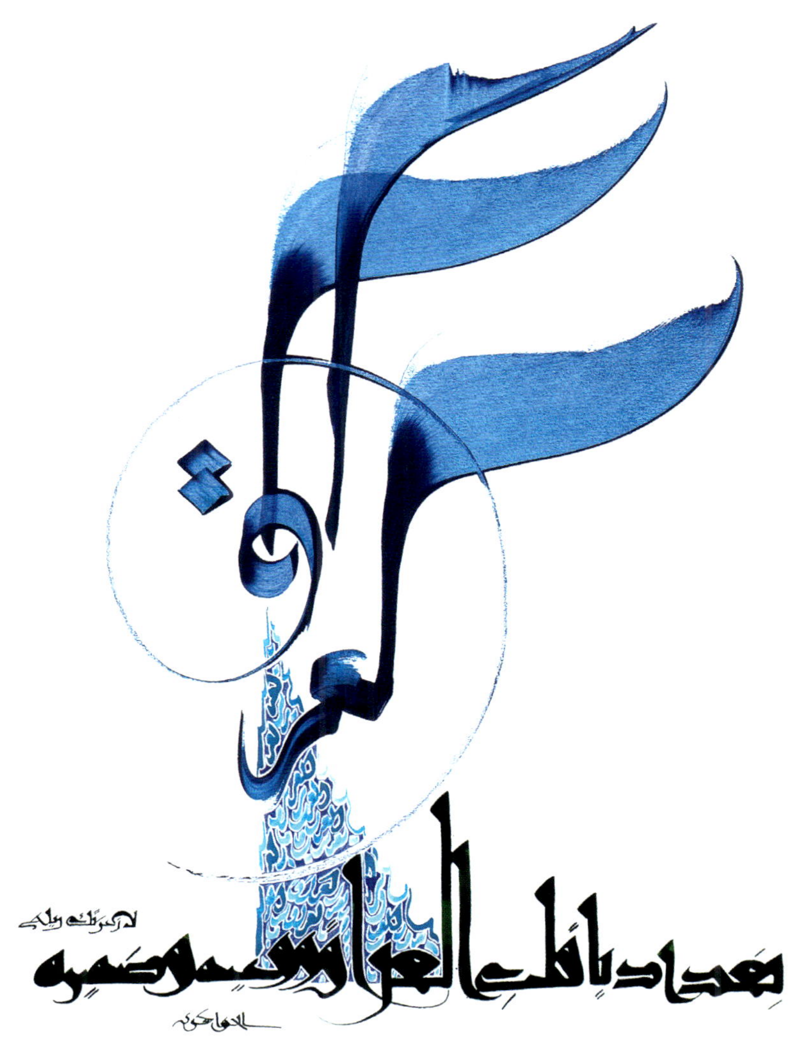

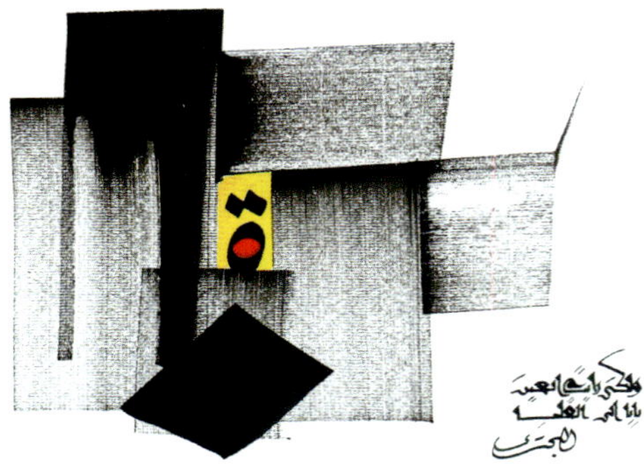

▲ ▶

I saw that the eye was
the window of the heart.

Al Buhturi (821–897)

ولكن رأيثُ العينَ باباً إلى القلبِ

البحتري

Bodies of water like horses
Breaking from the starter's rope
Hit the bath with a white
Roll of fluid ingots. Wind
Warms overhead creasing it.
The sun doubles its grimacing
Like an uncle. The rain adds
Gum and sorrow to the flow.
But at night the stars descend
In silent order, and you see
The cosmos standing on its hands.

Al Buhturi

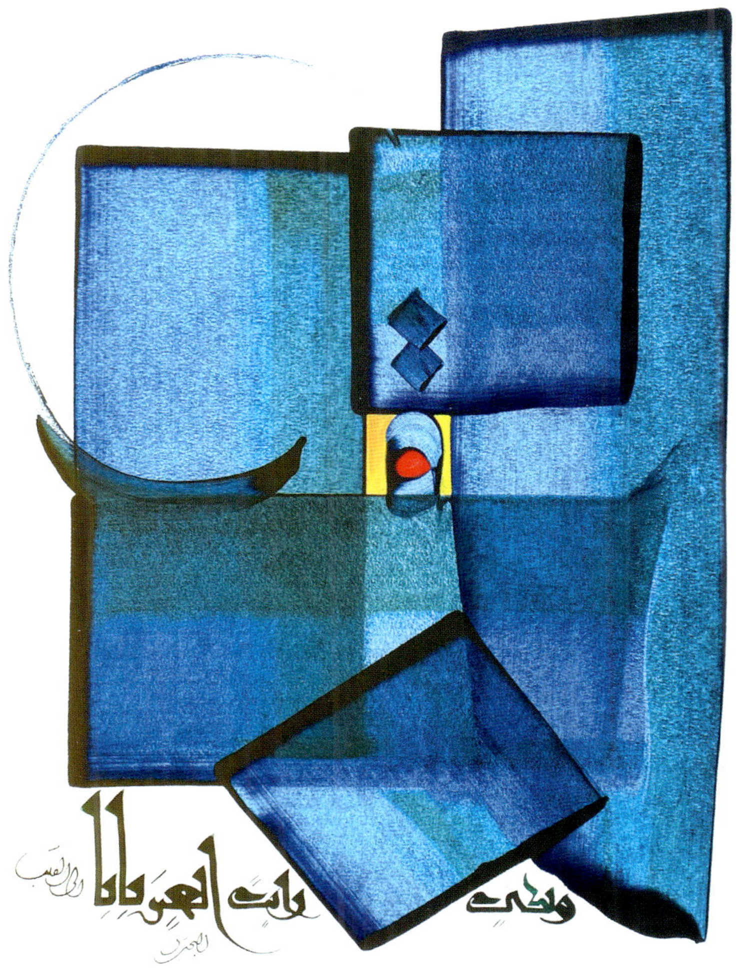

والضحى والليل إذا سجى ما ودعك ربك وما قلى

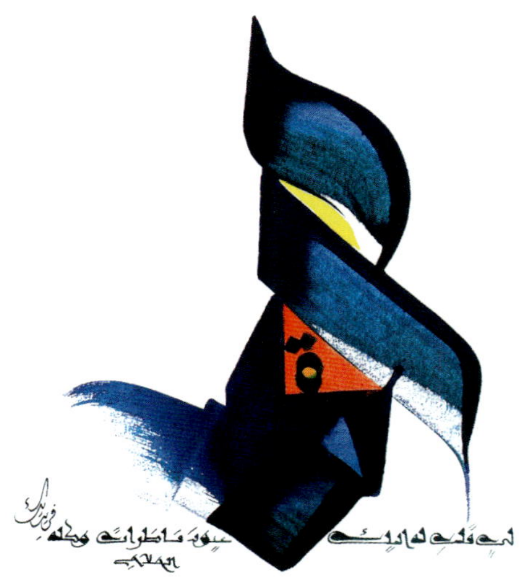

My heart has eyes only for you,
and is completely in your
hands.

Mansour al-Hallaj (858–922)

لي قلب له اليك عيون ناظرات
وكله بين يديك.
منصور الحلّاج

You are everything I am
My hearing and my sight,
My universe,
My trifling things.
The sum of everything I am
You are. And everything I am
Is mystery. I have confused you
With my little meaning.

Mansour al-Hallaj

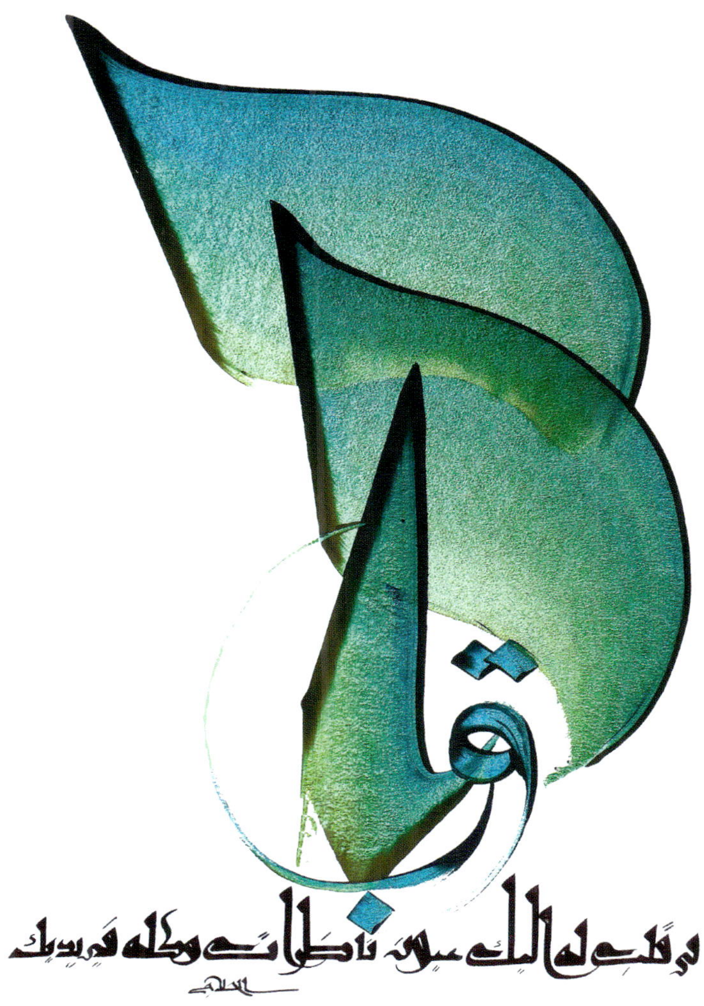

Man must make the effort to
progress by himself,
and not wait for destiny to play a
helping hand.

Kuthayyir (660–723)

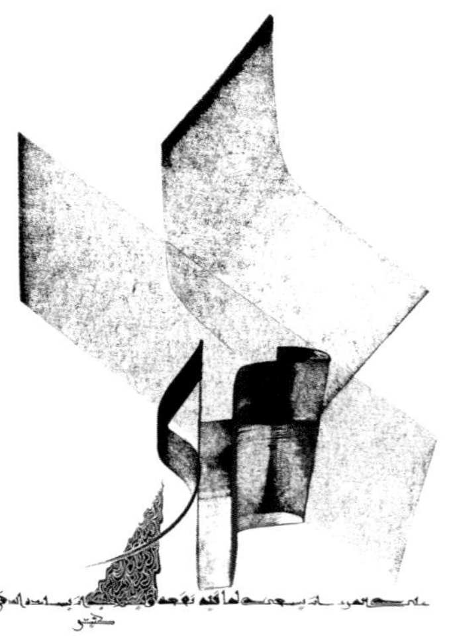

على المرءِ أن يسعى لما فيه نفعه
وليس عليه أن يساعَده الدَّهرُ
الشَّاعر كثيّر

By your life, there is no hardship on this earth for one
– be he desirous or monastic – who is reasonable.

Al-Shanfara (? –525)

لعمرك ما في الأرض ضيقٌ على امرِئٍ
سرى راغِباً أو راهِباً وهو يعقلُ
الشَّنفرى

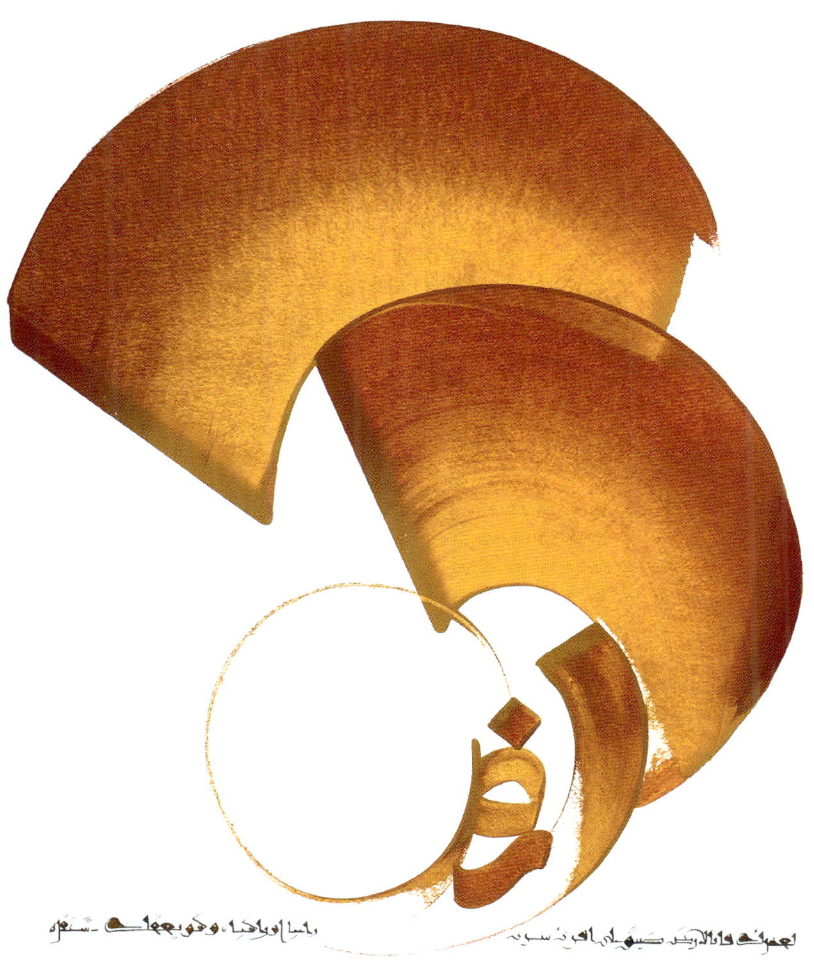
لعمرك ما الإنسان إلا ابن ... نسبه
رأسا واحدا، وكونهما ـ شعر

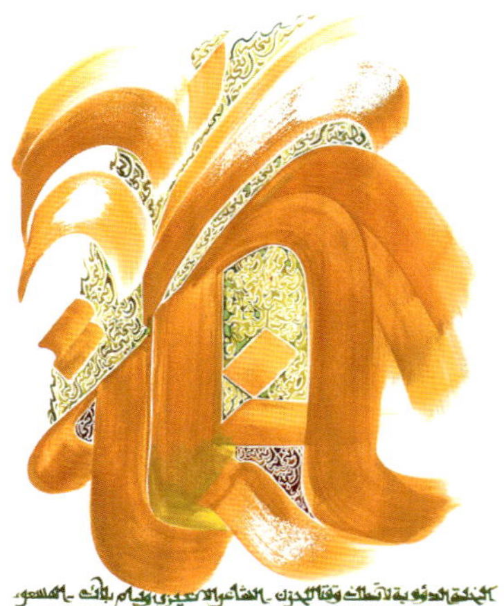

◀ ▶

The busy bee has no time to be despondent.

William Blake (1757–1827)

النّحلة الدّؤوبة لا تملك وقتاً للحزن.

وليام بلاك

To see a world in a grain of sand
And a Heaven in a wildflower,
Hold infinity in the palm of your hand
And eternity in an hour.
A robin red breast in a cage
Puts all Heaven in a rage
A dove house fill'd with doves and pigeons
Shudders Hell thr' all its regions.

William Blake

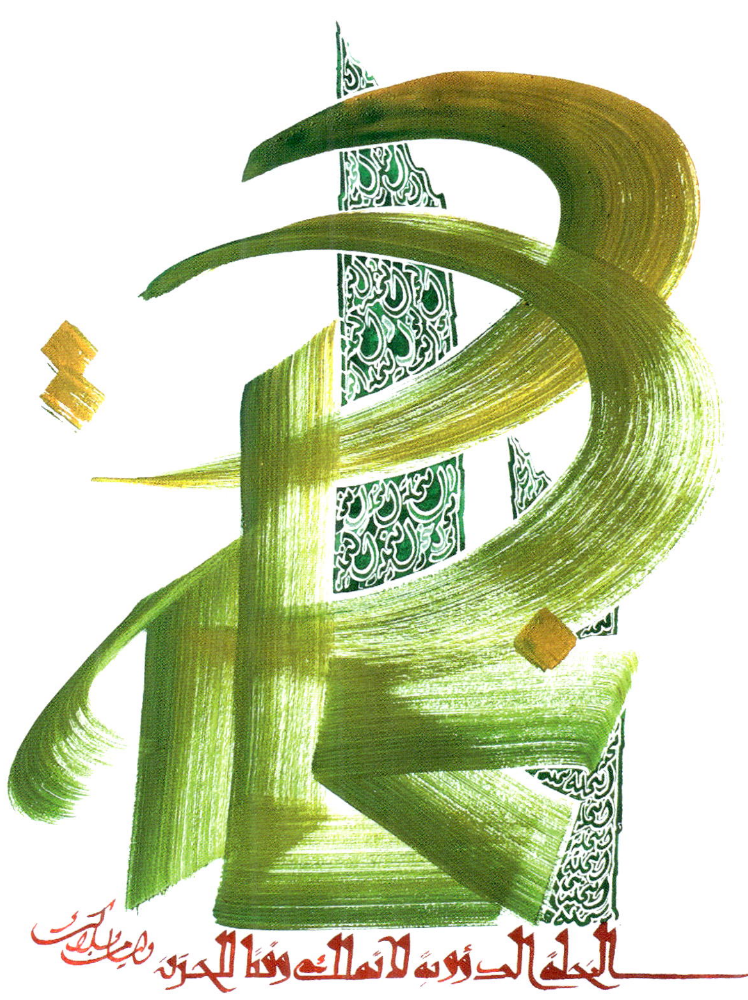

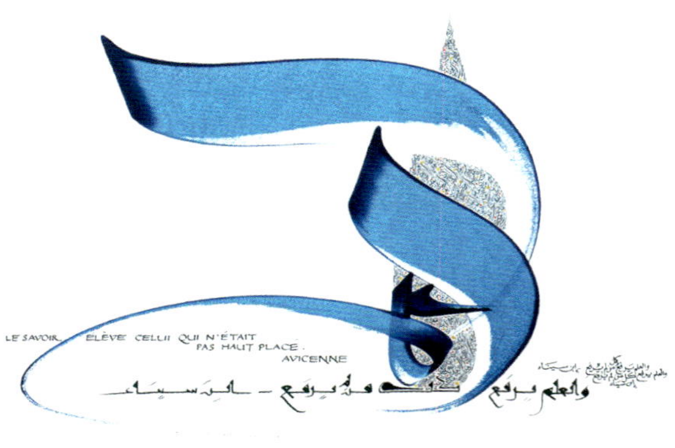

Knowledge nurtures a man who does not
have a high position.

Avicenna (980–1037)

والعلم يرفع كل من لم يرفع

ابن سينا

It descended upon thee from out of the regions above,
That exalted, ineffable, glorious, heavenly dove.
'Twas concealed from the eyes of all those
who its nature would ken,
Yet it wears not a veil and is apparent to men.
Unwilling it sought thee and joined thee, and ye, though it grieve,
It is still more unwilling thy body to leave.
It resisted and struggled, untamed to haste,
Yet it joined thee, and slowly grew used to this waste.

Avicenna

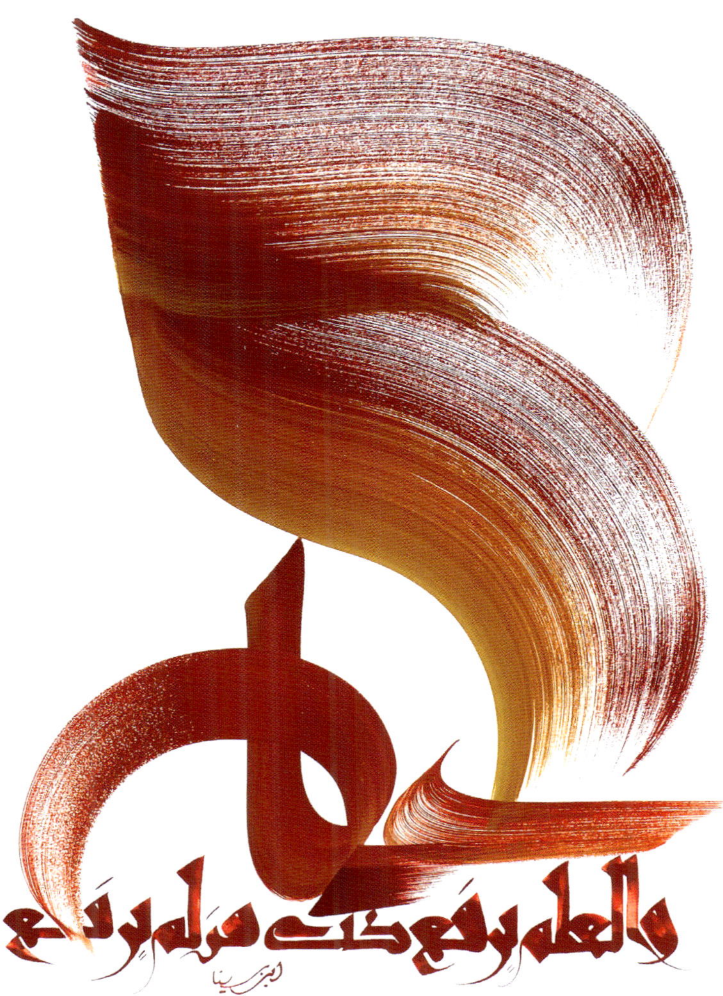

والعلم رفعة كل من لم يرفع
ابن سينا

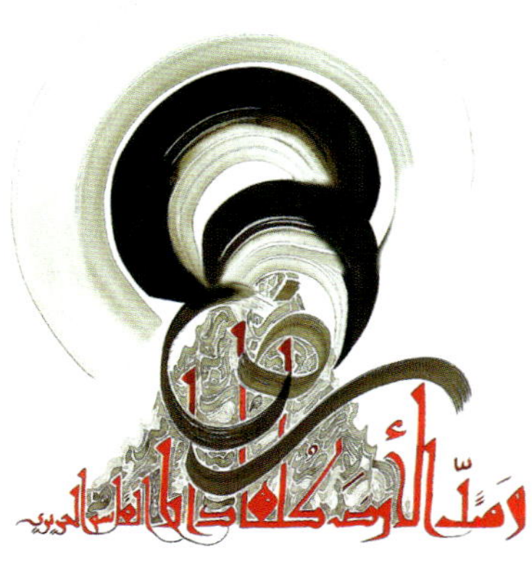

Imagine the whole earth as one home.

al-Qassim al-Hariri (1054–1122)

ومثل الأرض كلها دارا.

القاسم الحريري

I ride and I ride through the waste far and wide, and I fling
away pride to be gay as the swallow;
stem the torrent's fierce speed, tame the mettlesome steed,
that wherever I lead, youth and pleasure may follow.

al-Qassim al-Hariri

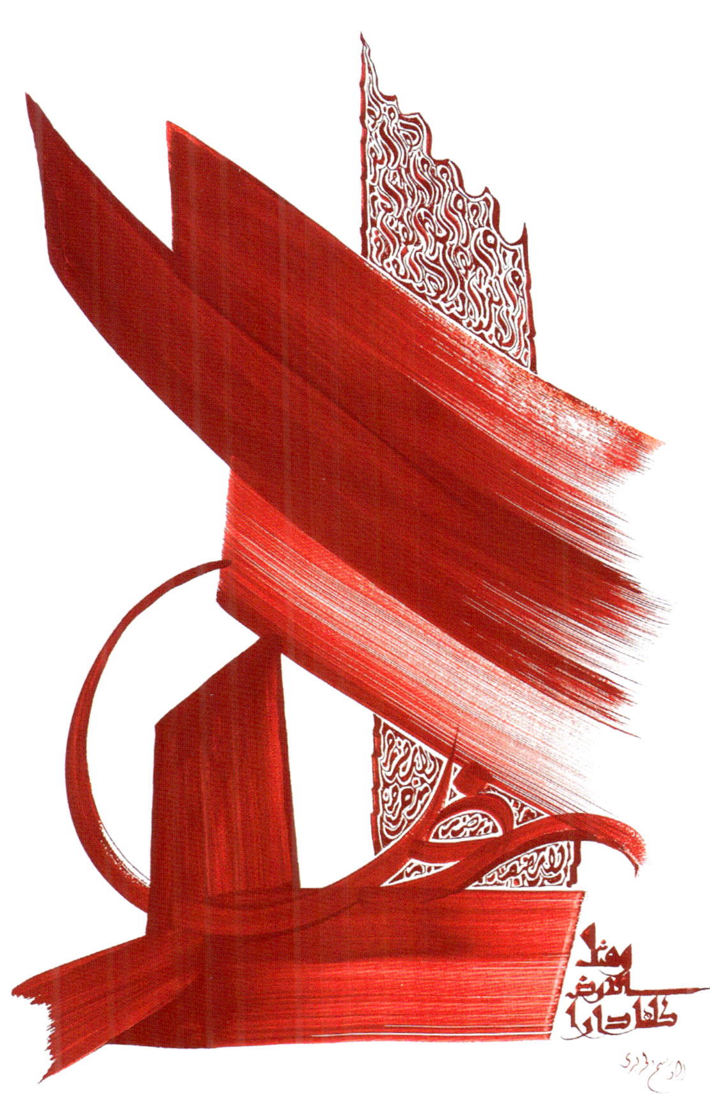

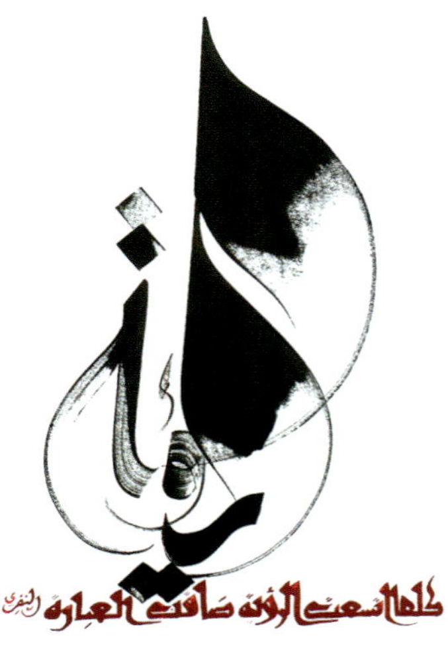

Whenever the vision is broadened, the words become narrowed.

al-Nifferi (10th c.)

كلّما اتّسعت الرؤية ضاقت العبارة.

النّفري

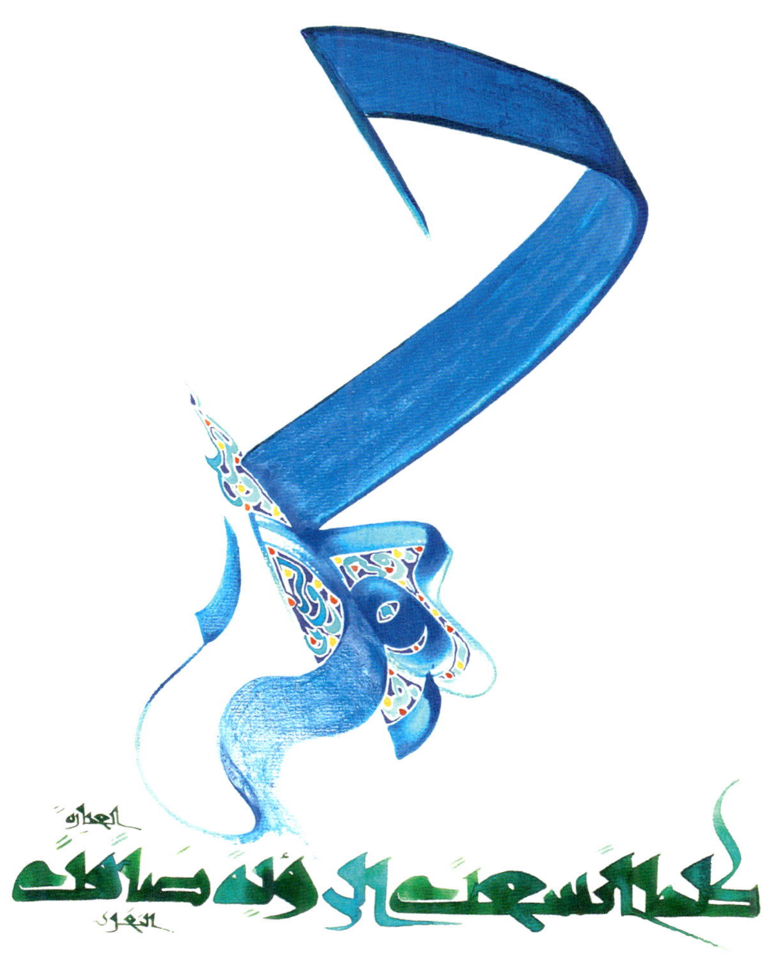

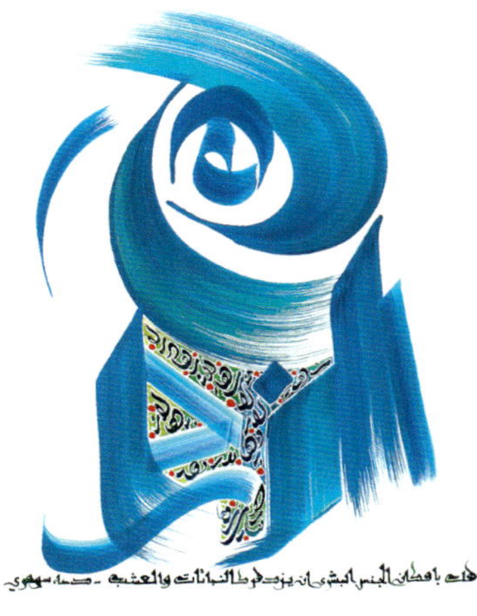

Can the human race prosper like
plants and grass?

Sumerian prayer

هل بإمكان الجنس البشري أن يزدهر
كالنّباتات والعشب؟

دعاء سومري

O woman: you are like clear water,
You are an ever-burning fire.
Were you to disappear, the earth would wither,
And all that is good would be gone.

Sumerian prayer

أيّتها المرأة، أنتِ كالمياه العذبة،
أنتِ النّار التي لا تنطفئ.
ان غبتِ تذبل الأرض
ويُمحى الخير عن الوجود.

دعاء سومري

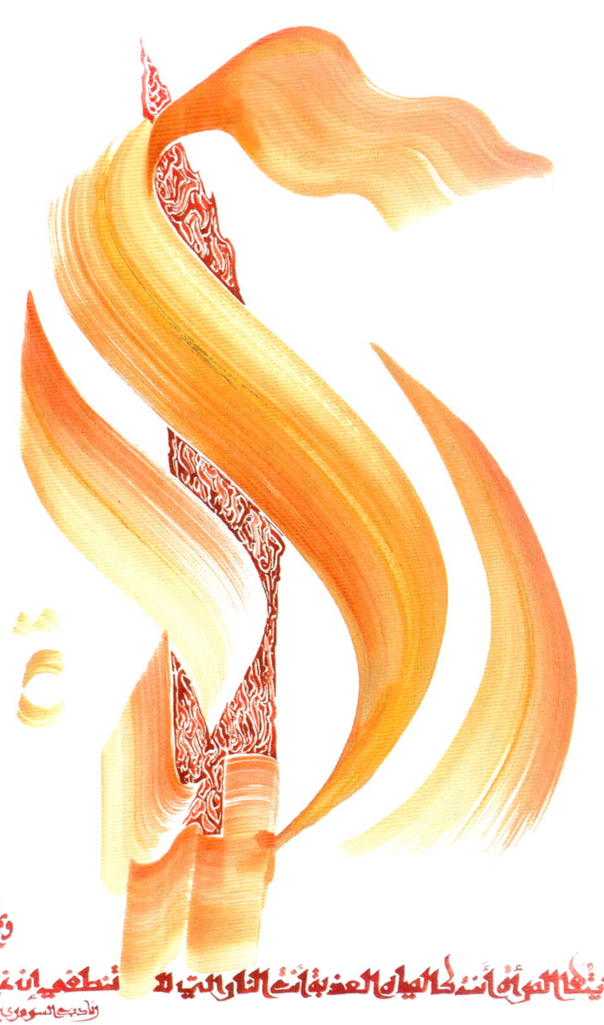

ويمحى الخير عن الصمود
أيتها المرأة أنت كالمياه العذبة أنت النار التي لا تنطفئ إن نبت تذبل الأرض
نادبة السومري - العراق القديم

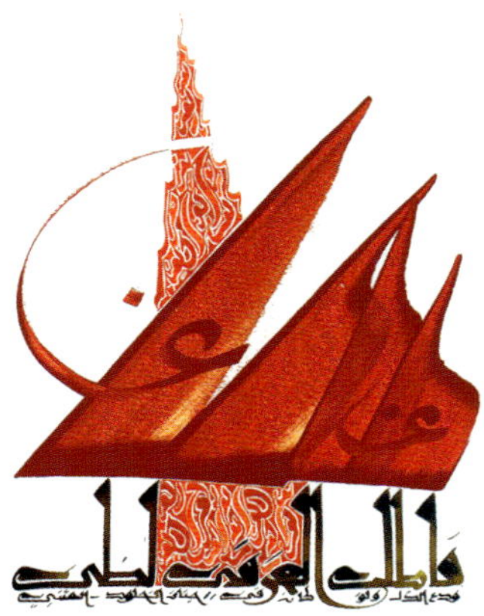

Strive for dignity even in hell, and
refuse humiliation even in paradise.

al-Mutanabbi (915–965)

وأطلب العز في لظى ودع الذل
ولوْ كان في جنان الخلودِ.
المتنبّي

If my will fade for distant fear,
it fades too for chances near.

al-Mutanabbi

إذا فل عزمي مدى خوف بعده
فأقرب شيء ممكن لم يجد عزما
المتنبي

Parting has just taught our eyelids separation
That bleeds, and associated the heart with grief.
I hoped the hour they went for a show of her wrist
So the tribe perplexed would stay before going
If she appeared to bewilder them shame would draw
A curtain to guard their wits from her glance.
By the camel and its driver and myself! A moon
Is panting in the curtains from her motion.

al-Mutanabbi

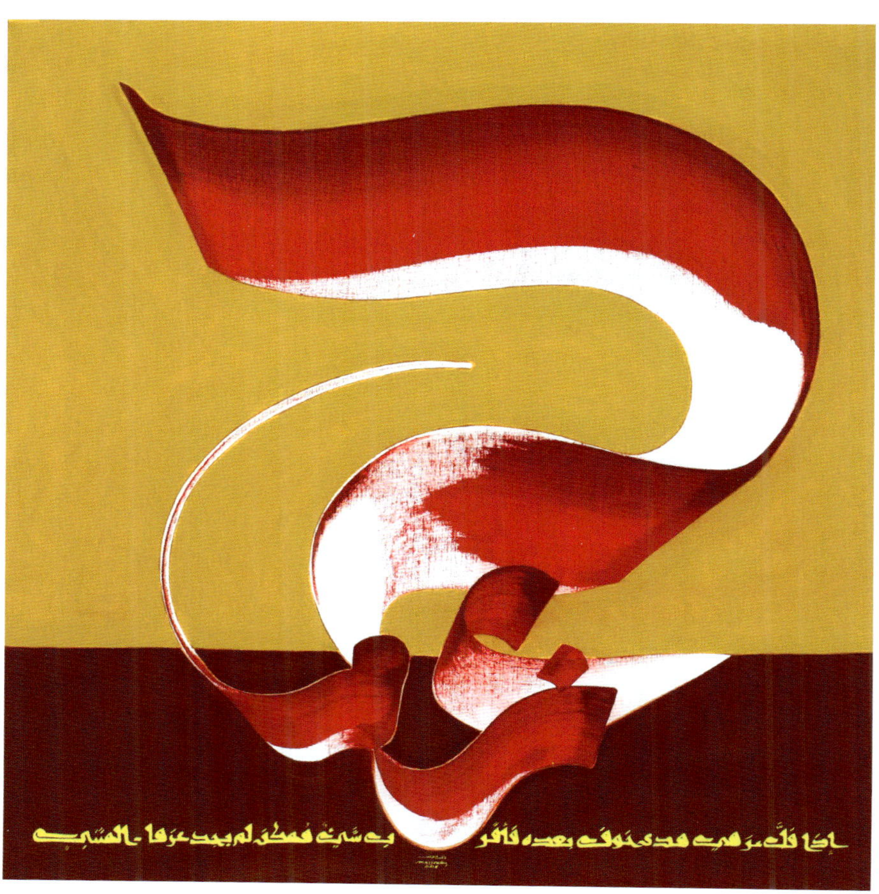

إذا قل مرء قد خدعوك بعده تأثر بعد شيء فمكنه لم يجد عرفا - المتنبي

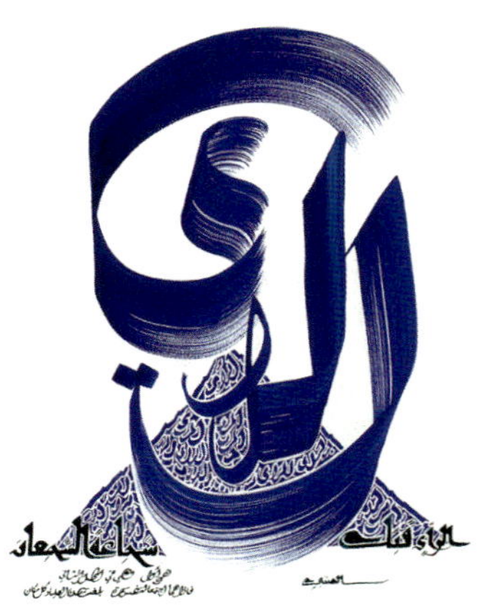

▲

According to men's wills strength
comes, noble acts come in respect to
their bounty.

al-Mutanabbi (915–965)

الرأي قبل شجاعة الشجعان،
هو أول وهي في المحل الثاني.
المتنبي

►

Courage to reason second place must take
For valour should not balanced judgment shake
But if both in hard soul united are
Then glory's realms their own demesne shall make.

al-Mutanabbi

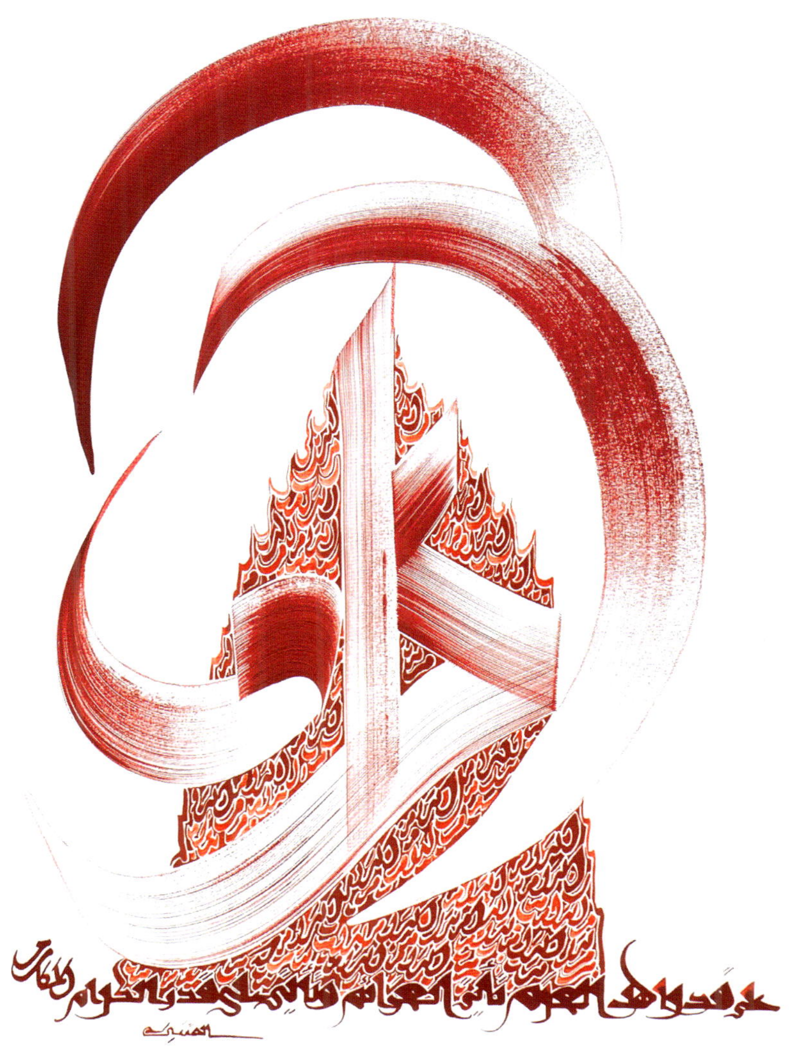

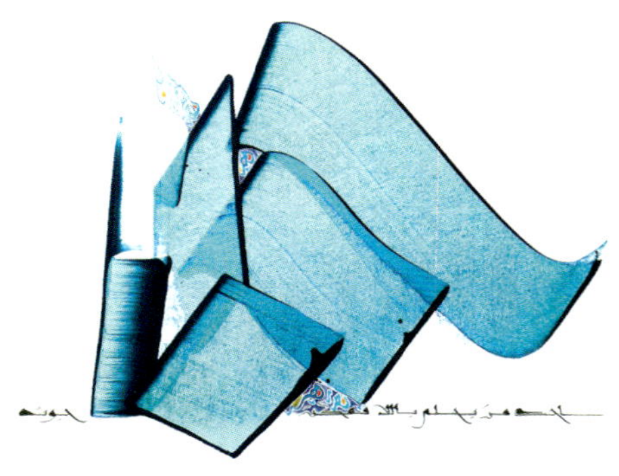

▲

I love him who desires impossibilities.
Enter! Thou bold one, thou shalt rejoice!
This dark way leads to Proserpine.
In the hollow base of Olympus,
she listens in secret for forbidden greeting.

Johann Wolfgang von Goethe (1749–1832)

أحبّ من يحلم باللاممكن.
يوهان فولفغانغ فون غوته

▶

Life and joy culminate where beauty reigns.

Friedrich von Schiller (1759–1805)

الحياة والفرح يلتقيان حيث يعم الجمال.
فريدريش فون شيلر

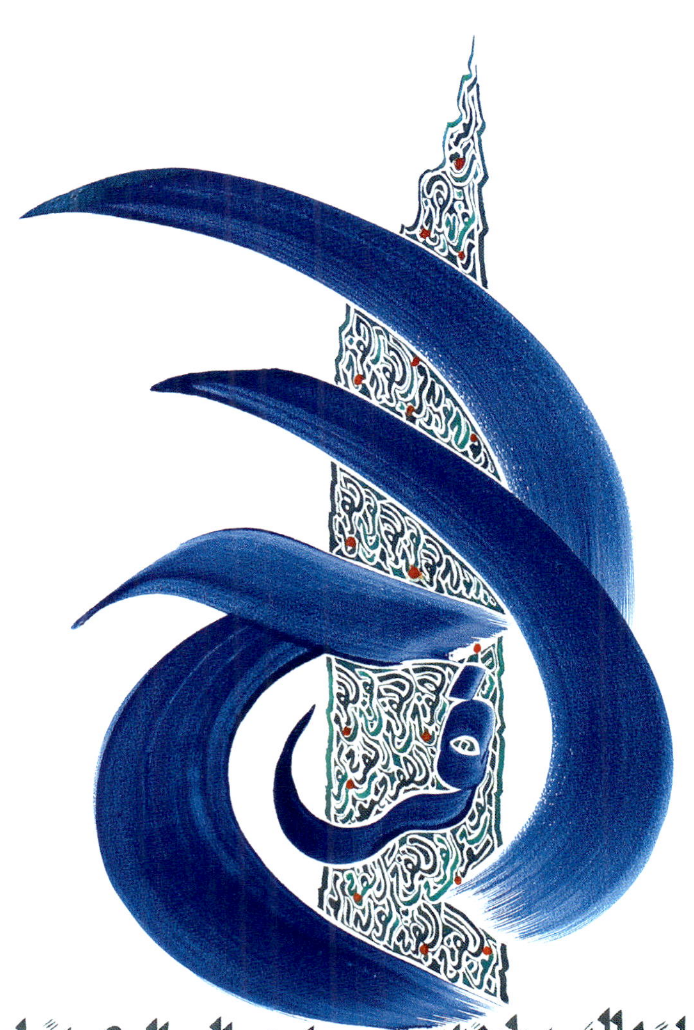

الحياة والهوى بلهناء عند ما يعم الحراك - سيلو

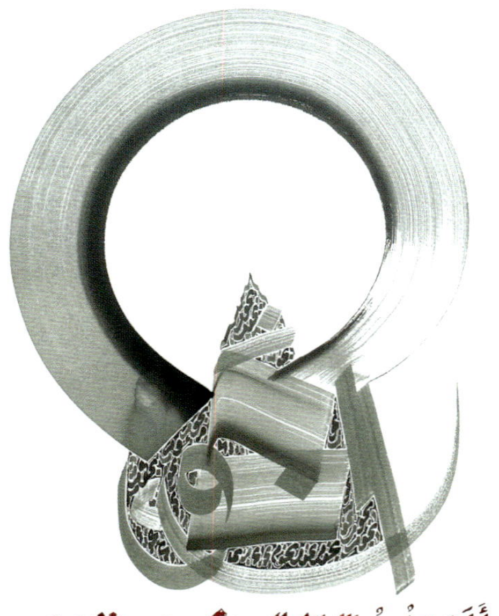

▲ ▶

I will pay attention to the stars of the
night, for the love of a full moon.

Ibn Khafaja (1058–1135)

أراعي نجوم الليل حبّاً لبدره
ابن خفاجة

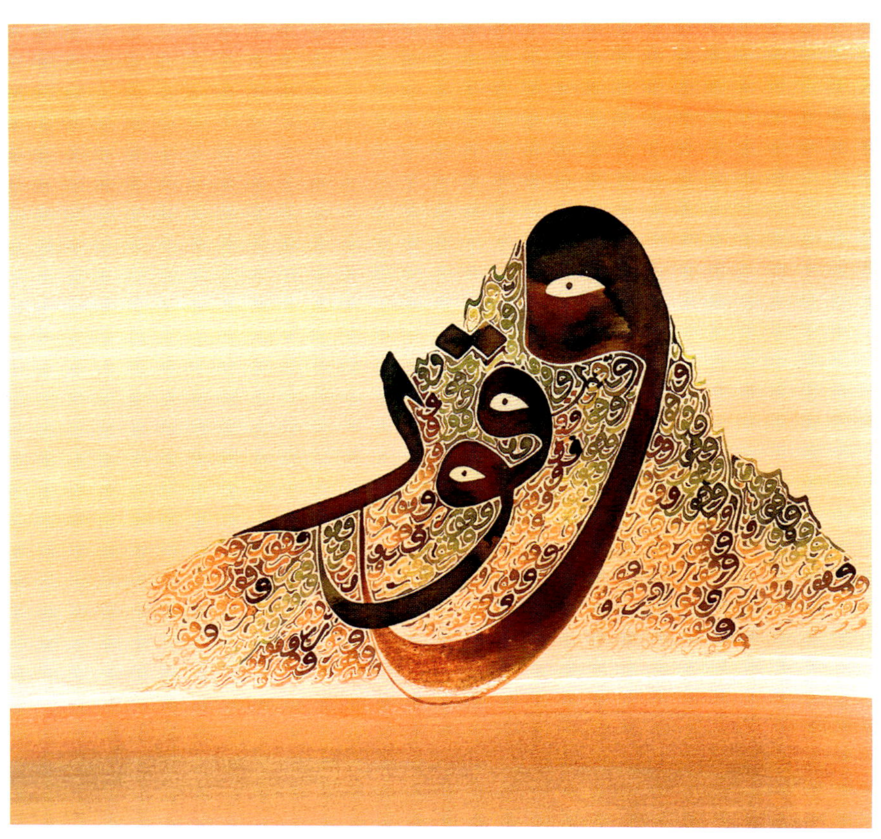

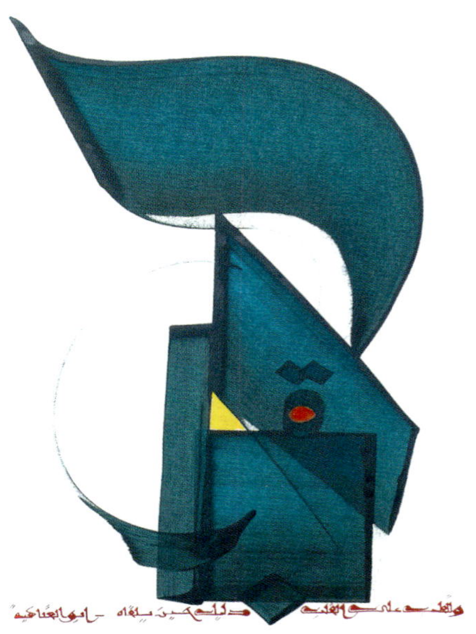

▲ ▶

The heart is a guide for the heart
as soon as they meet.

Abu al-Attahia (751–832)

وللقلب على القلب
دليلٌ حين يلقاه
أبو العتاهية

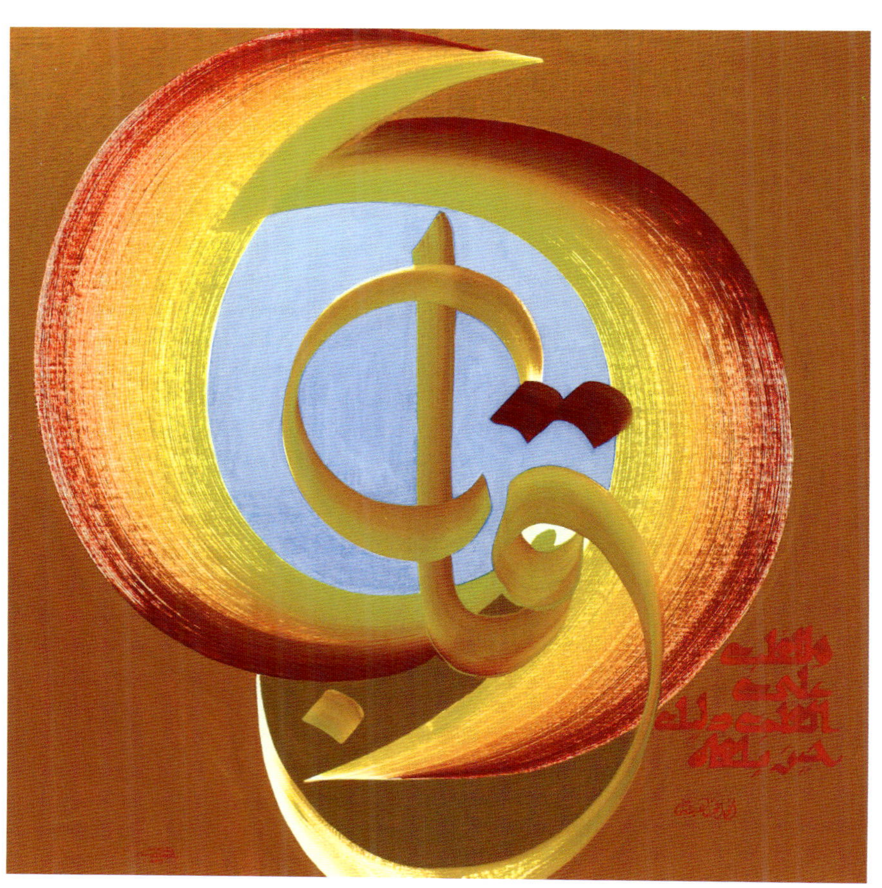

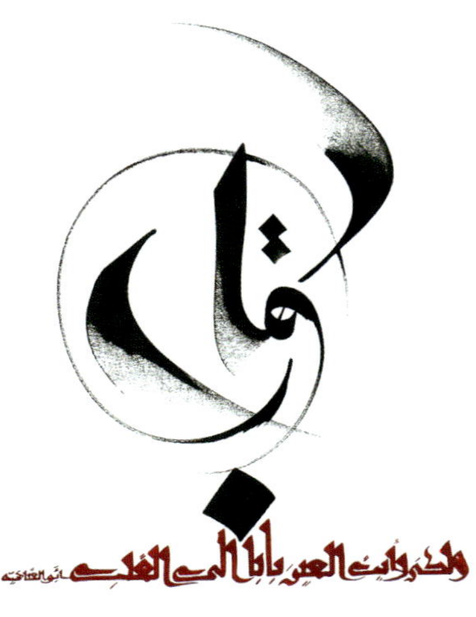

I saw the eye was the window to the heart

Al Buhturi (821–897)

ولكني رأيت العين بابا الى القلب

البحتري

Everytime the crescent moon rises
I recall my life; I rejoice whenever
the crecent moon appears.

Abu al-Attahia (748-825)

يمر بي الهلال لهدم عمري

وأفرح كلما طلع الهلال

أبو العتاهية

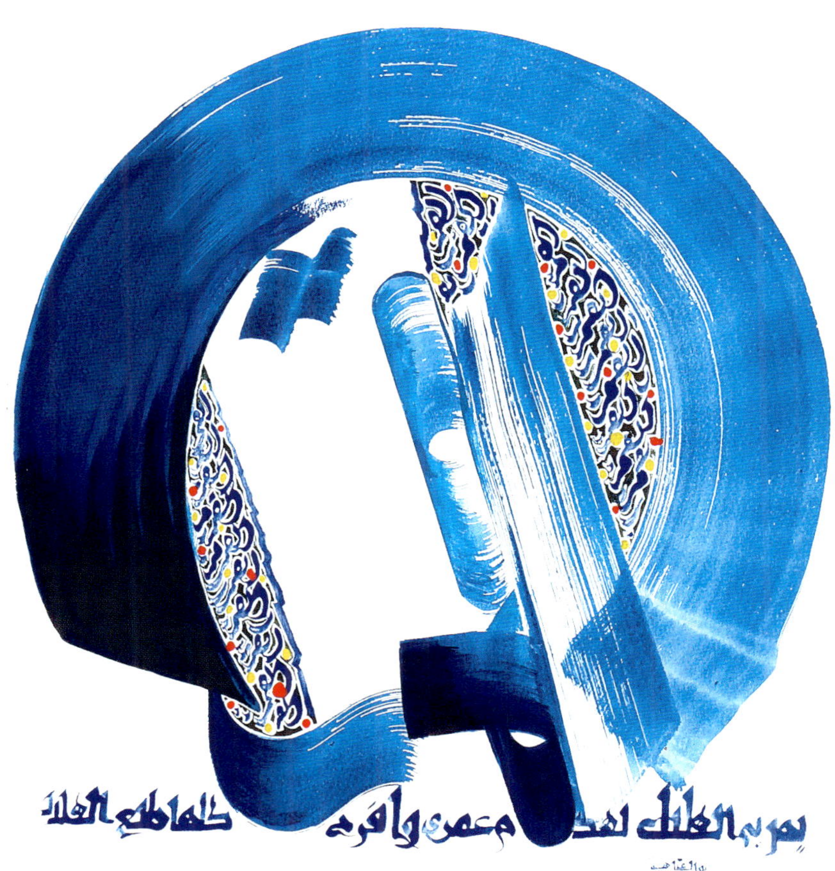

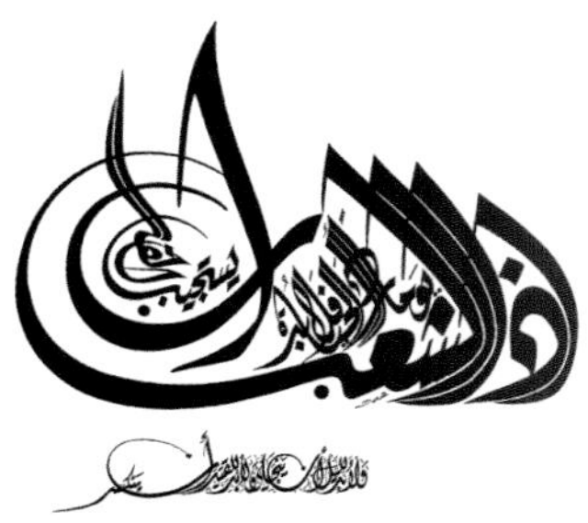

◄

When one day the people want to live,
Fate is forced to respond ...

Abu al-Qasim al-Shabbi (1909–1934)

►

The light is in my heart and between
my wings, so why am I afraid to walk in
darkness.

Abu al-Qasim al-Shabbi

النّور في قلبي وبينَ جوانحي
فعلامَ أخشى السّير في الظّلماء
أبو القاسم الشّابي

Those with no love for scaling mountains
Live forever in the ditches.
The blood of youth spurs on my heart
A new wind roars in my chest
So I bow my head, and listen
To the clap of thunder, the wind-song,
The sound of falling rain.

Abu al-Qasim al-Shabbi

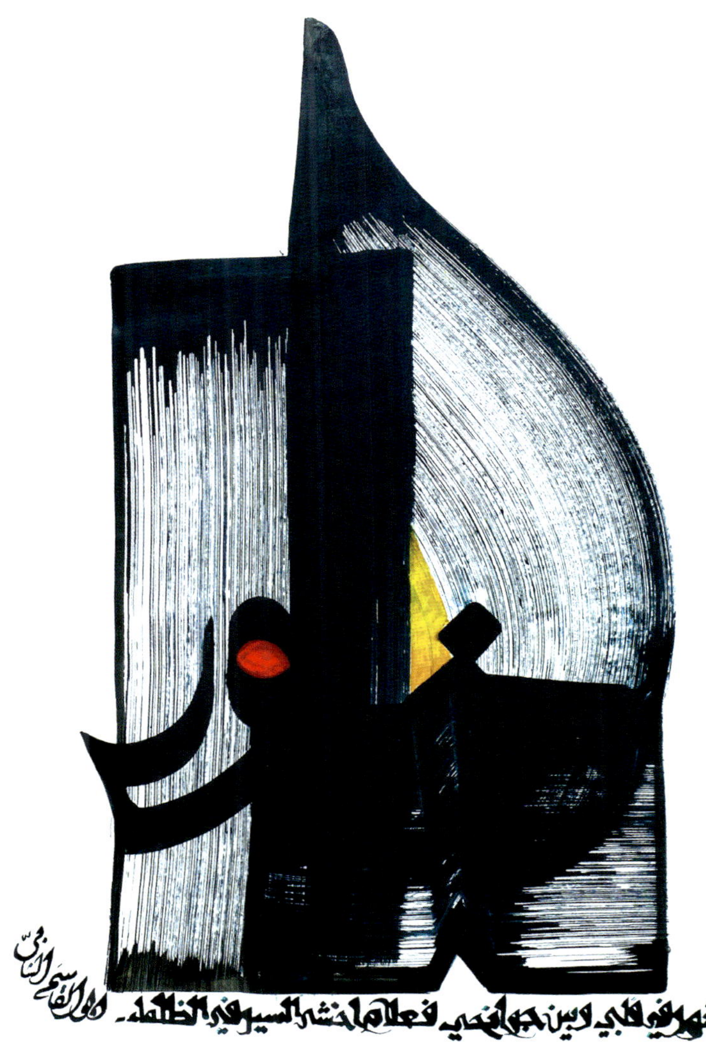

النور في قلبي وبين جوانحي فعلام أخشى السير في الظلمة ـ
هلال القاسم الشابي

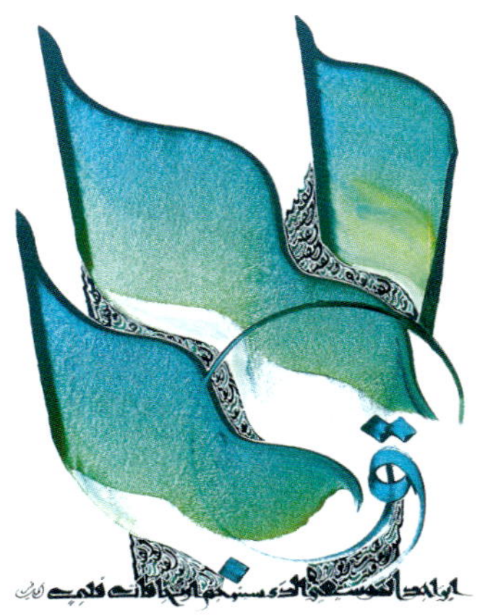

▲

Where can you find a beauty that lends – for a moment – an ear
To the moan of a heart that cherishes its pain?
Who, each time she wrinkles my heart
Will adorn her two amber-scented tresses with a new curl,
Who will soothe the burning of my heart in the coolness of wine
And drown hell in the river of Paradise.
Where can I find a musician to translate the turmoil of my heart
To the rhythm of the flute?

Urfi Shirazi (1555–1591)

أين أجد الموسيقي الذي سيترجم ارتجافات قلبي؟
عرفي الشيرازي

▶

The darkest night has a bright end.

Nizami (1141–1209)

الليلة الأكثر ظلاماً لها نهاية مضيئة.
نظامي

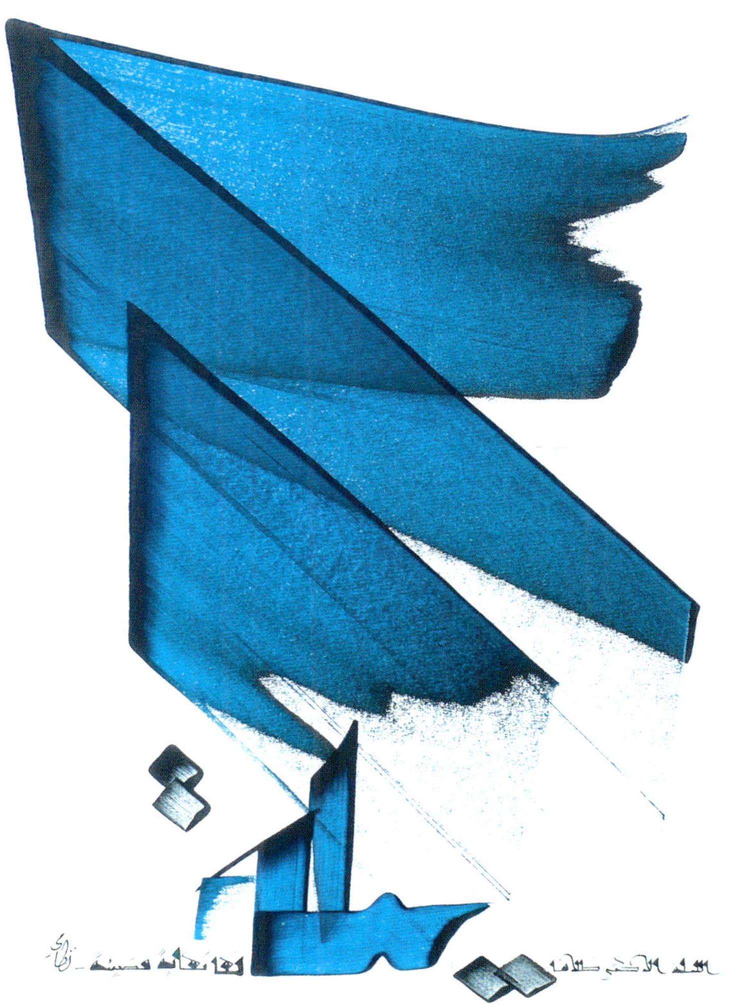

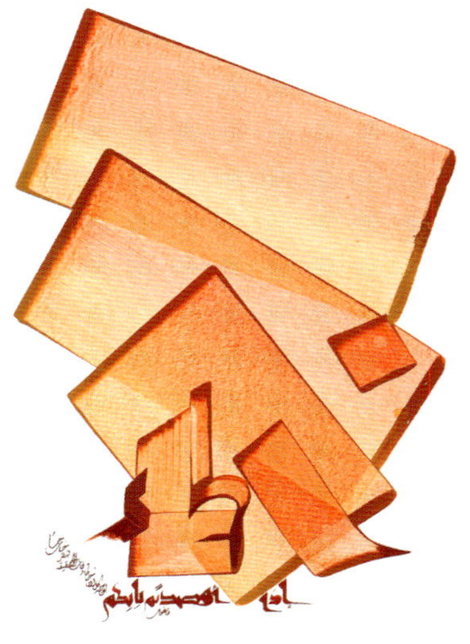

If you shut your door to all
errors, truth will be shut out.

Rabindranath Tagore (1861–1941)

إذا اوصدتم بابكم امام كل الأخطاء
فأن الحقيقة تبقى خارجا.
طاغور

The East and West are ever in search of each other,
and must eventually meet.

Rabindranath Tagore

لا يني ينشد الشرق والغرب أحدهما الآخر ولا بدّ أن يلتقيا.
طاغور

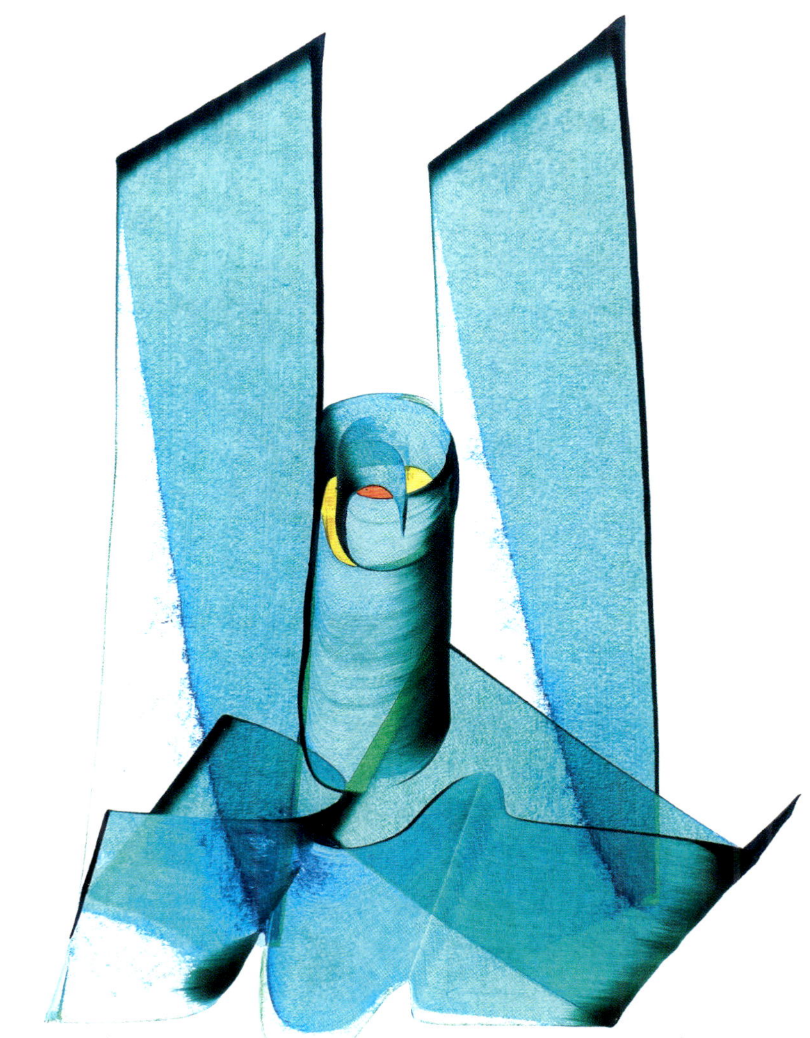

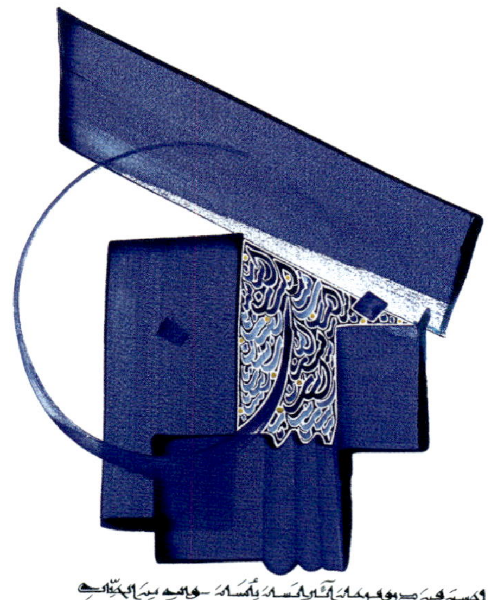

Better than pearls and coral is the gesture of
one man towards another man.

Walibah ibn al-Habbab (8th c.)

أحسن من درّ ومرجان
آثار إنسان بإنسان
والبة بن الحباب

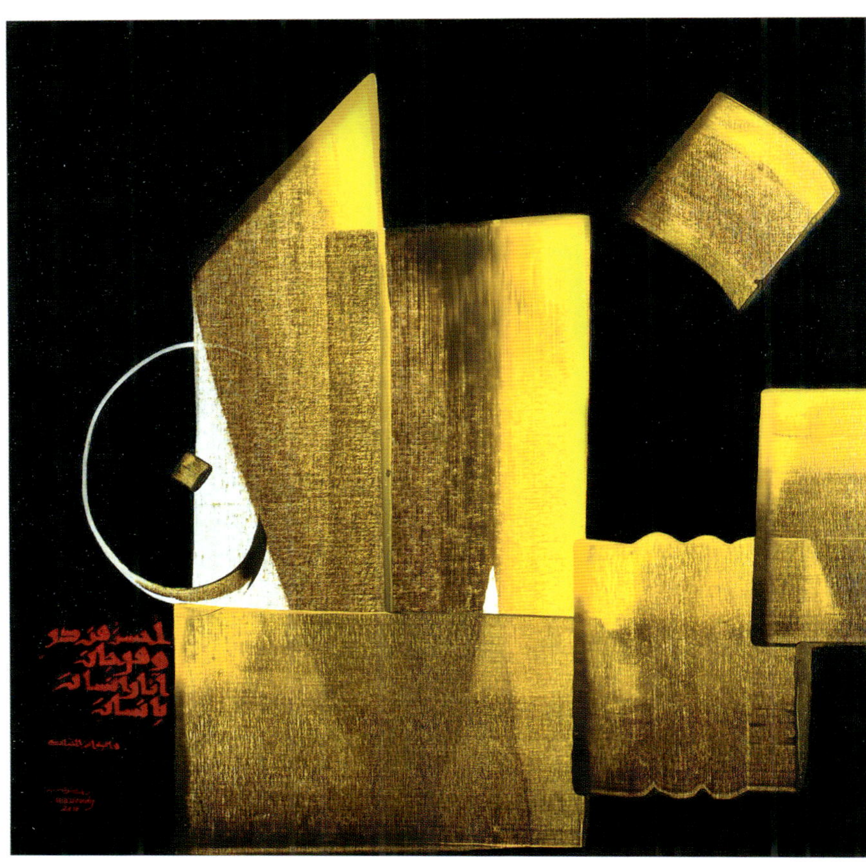

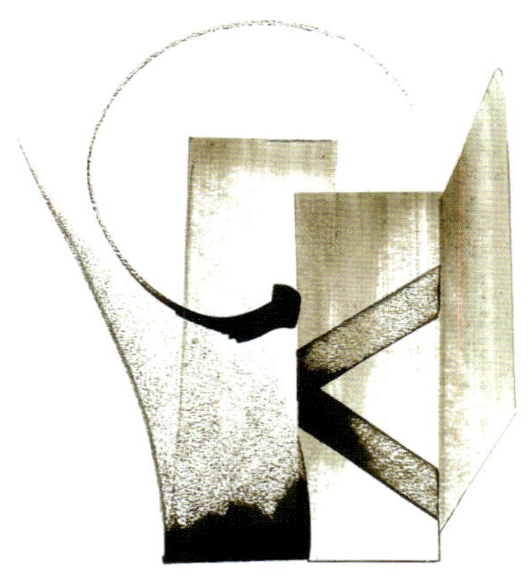

The best of speech is
concise and precise.

Ibn al-Suli (880–946)

وخير الكلام ماقل ودل.
عن كتاب الصولي

Don't use two words where one will do.

Ibn al-Suli

لا تنفق كلمتين إذا كفتك كلمة.
أبو بكر الصولي

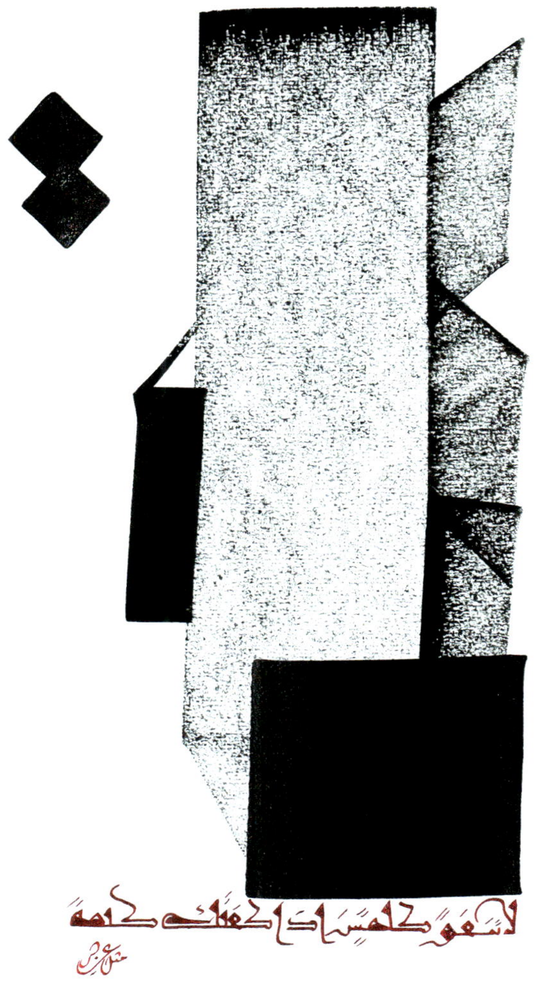

Give us wings to open the horizons of ascent,
to break free from our confined cavern, the solitude
of iron walls.

Give us light, to pierce the deepest darkness
And with the strength of its brilliant flow
We will push our steps to a precipice
From which to reap life's victories.

Fadwa Tuqan (1917–2003)

▶

Give us love
So that we may take the crumbling world
And build it within ourselves, anew.

Fadwa Tuqan

أعطنا حباً فنبني العالم المنهار فينا من جديد.

فدوى طوقان

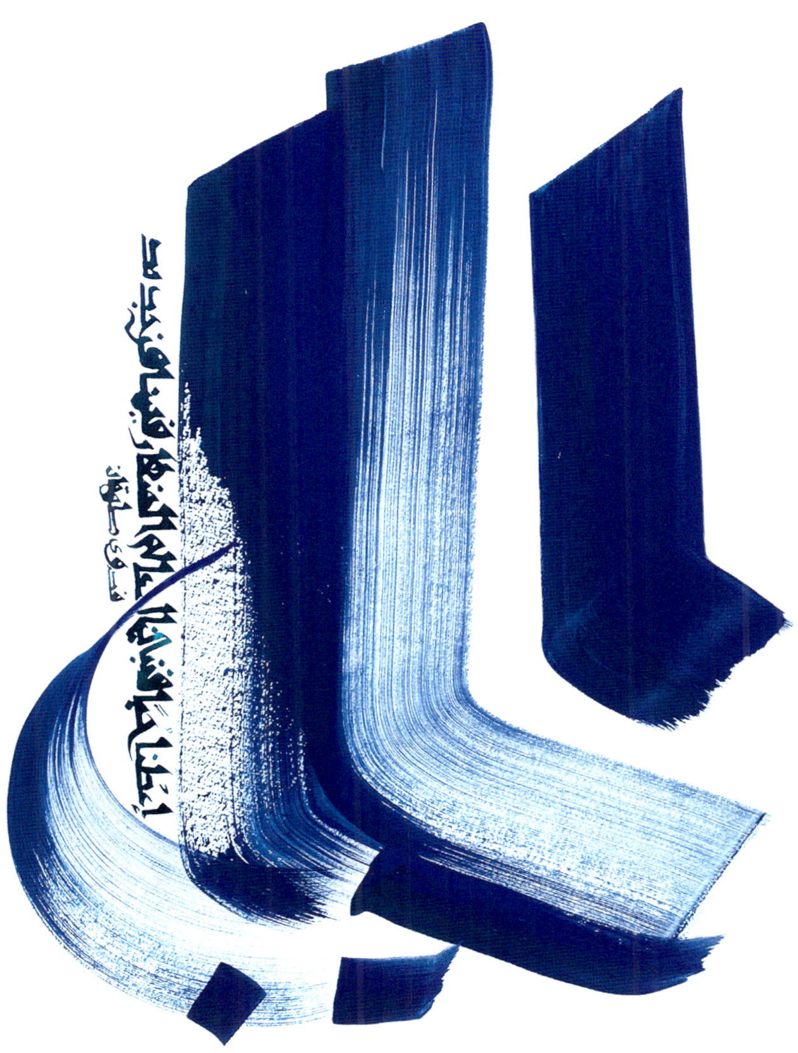

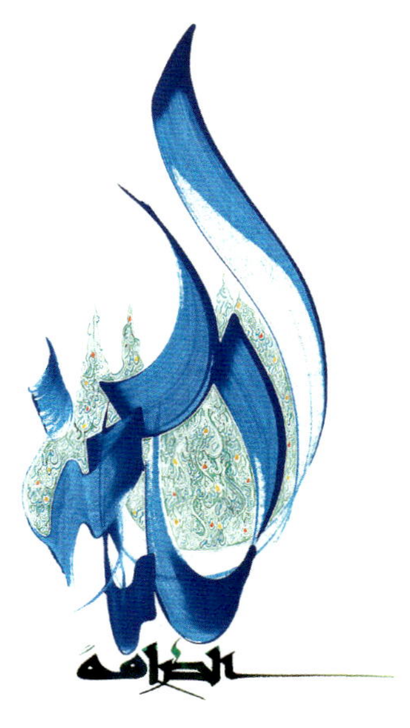

Before falling asleep, I dream of
peace returning to Earth and
happiness to people.

Samih al-Qasim (1939–2014)

واحلم قبل النوم مرّة،
ليعود للأرض السلام،
وتعود في الناس المسرّة.
سميح القاسم

Dignity

الكرامة

An hour from now
The sun will end its repose
And melt the snow
Sweeping lilies down to the meadow.

Samih al-Qasim

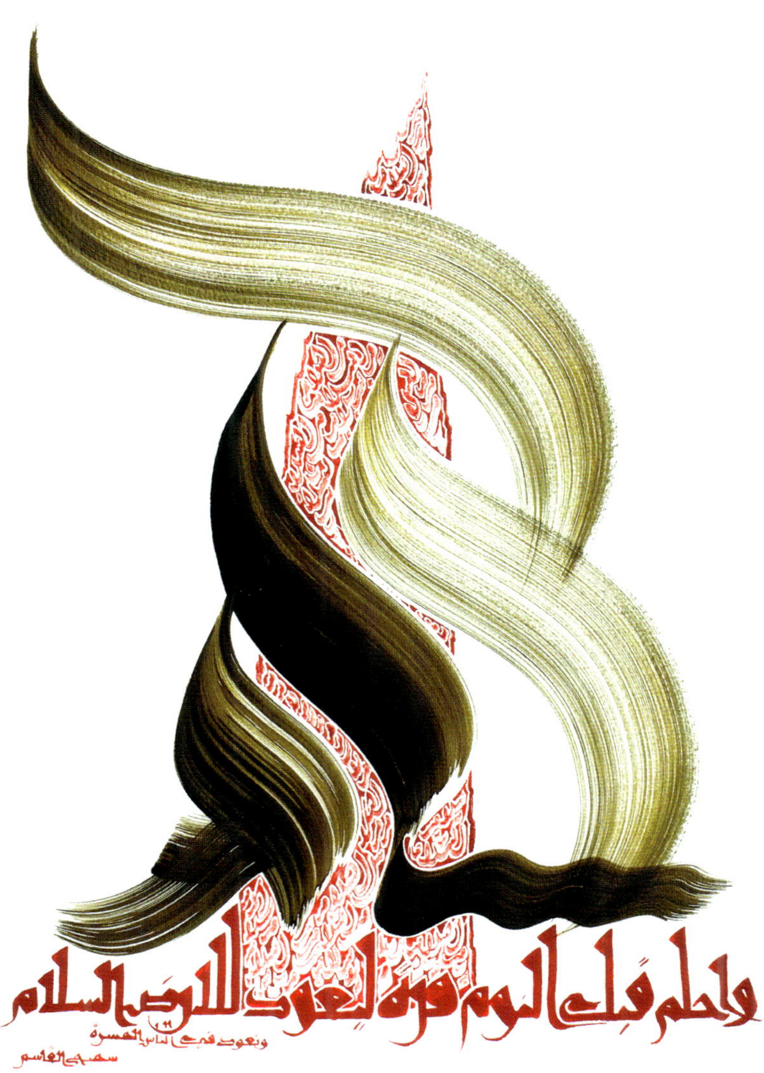

وأحلم ملء النوم فيه لنعود للأرض السلام
ونعود فنمسح دمع الناس الحسرة
سميح القاسم

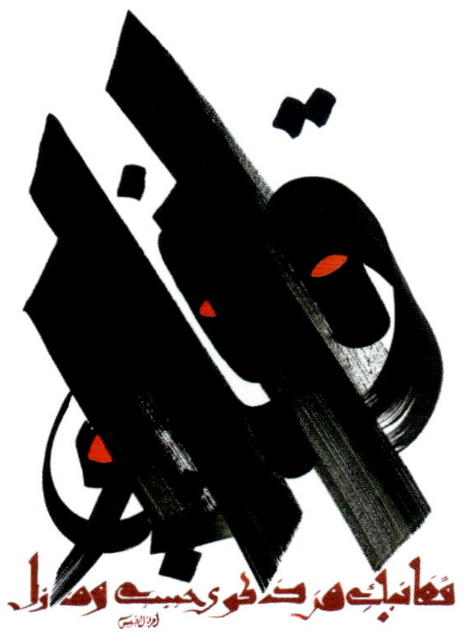

As my companions halt their steeds,
They say, 'stay strong, don't give in to sorrow.'

Imru al-Qays (501–544)

وقوفا بها صحبي علي مطيهم
يقولون : لاتهلك أسى و تجمل.
امرؤ القيس

For me, life is a treasure which every night fades away;
never do the days stop and life is slowly consumed.

Tarafa ibn al-Abd (543–569)

أرى العيش كنزاً ناقصاً كلّ ليلة
وما تنقص الأيام والدهر ينفد
طرفة بن العبد

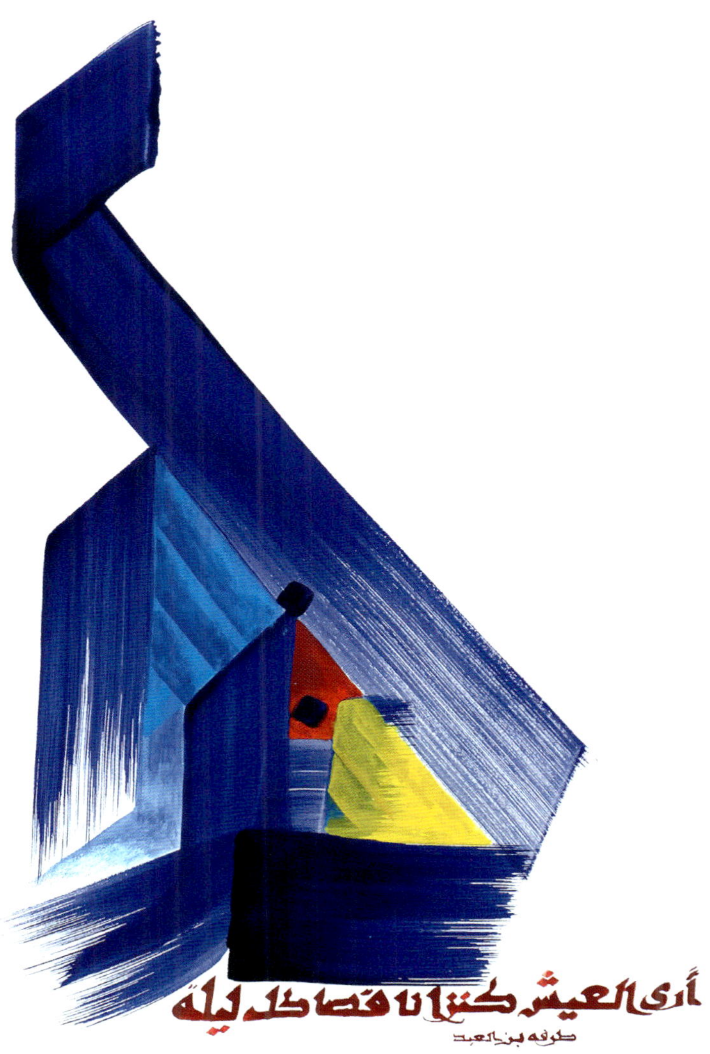

أرى العيش كنزاً ناقصاً كل ليلة
طرفة بن العبد

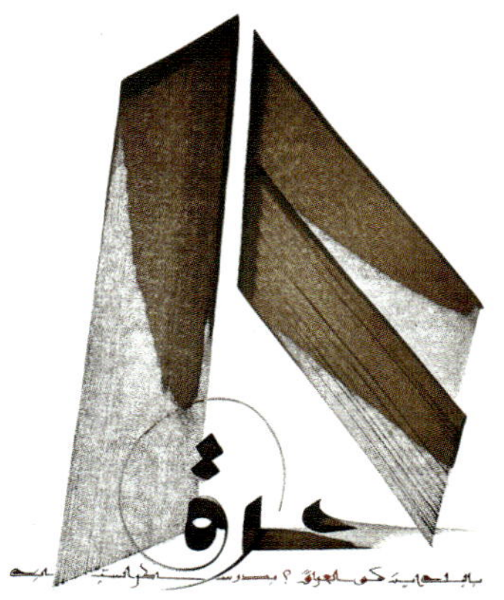

Oh night! Where are you Iraq?

Badr Shakir al-Sayyab
(1926–1964)

يا ليل أين هو العراق؟
بدر شاكر السيّاب

Your eyes: as if stars pulsed in their depths
Drowning in sorrow's gauzy mist
Like a sea tousled by hands of night,
With warmth of winter, shiver of fall,
Death and birth, darkness and light;
My spirit awakens, trembles with tears
Wild delight embraces the sky
Like a frantic child afraid of the moon.
An arch of cloud slakes its thirst with the mist
And drop by drop, passes into rain.
Children laughing in the vinyards
Silent birds in the trees, roused by the
Song of the rain.

Badr Shakir al-Sayyab

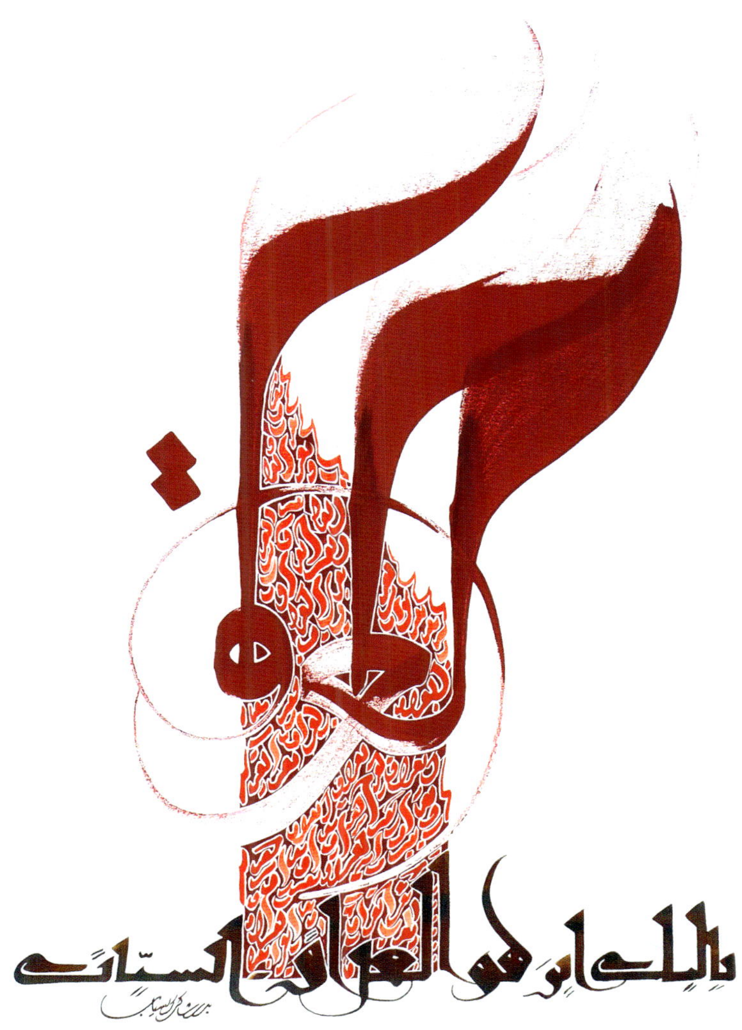

بالله ائذن في العالم الإنساني

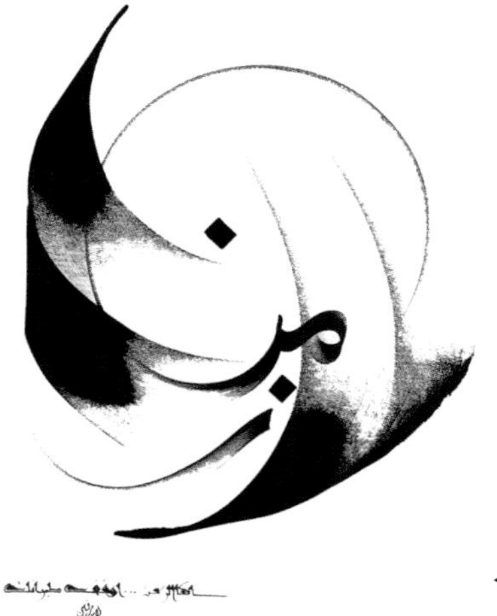

◀ ▶

Oh time, arrest your flight!

Alphonse de Lamartine
(1790–1869)

أيّها الزّمن، أوقف طيرانَك.
ألفونس دو لامارتين

O time, arrest your flight, and you, propitious hours!
Suspend your course:
Let us savour the swift delights
Of the most beautiful of our days!

Alphonse de Lamartine

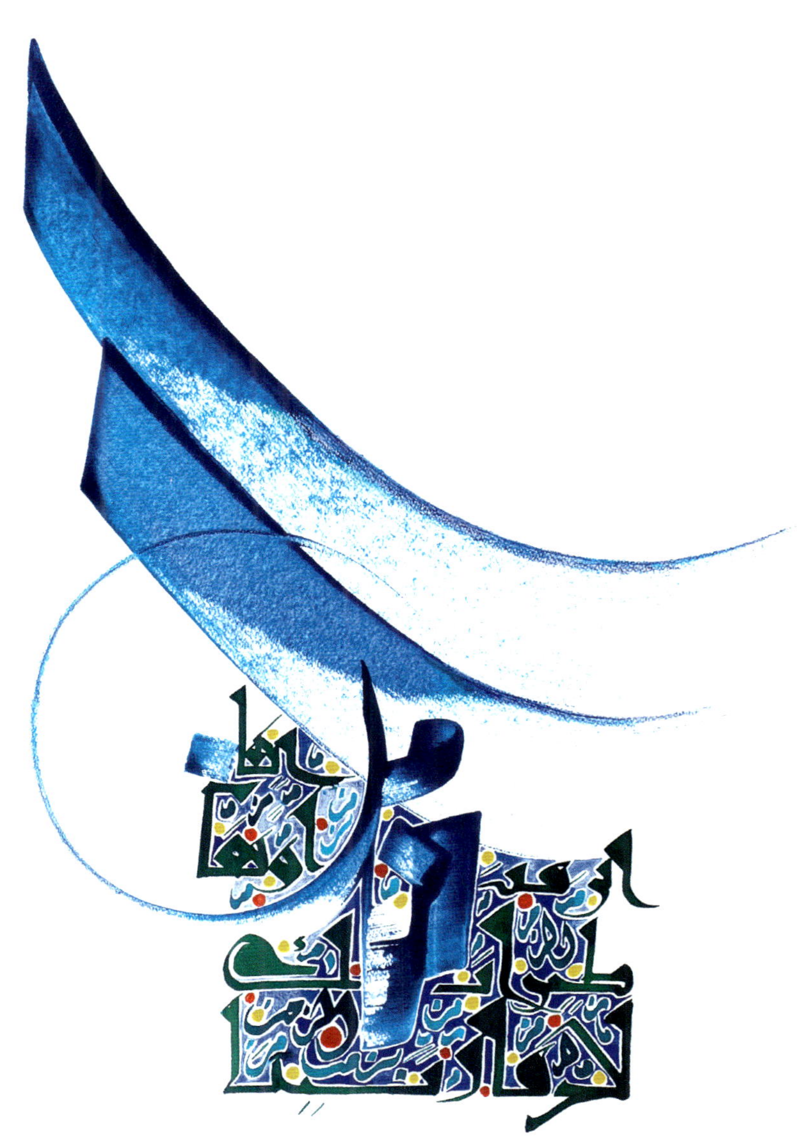

CITATIONS

The texts found on these pages were originally published in the following collections:

11 al-Sheer we al-Shuara, Dar Altakafa, volume 1 by Ibn Qutaybah; 14, 16 Rubai'yât by Jalal al-Din Rumi; 20, 22 Revolt Against The Sun by Nazik al-Mala'ika (Saqi Books); 28 Capitale de la Douleur by Paul Éluard; 30 Umar b. al-Farid Poèmes mystiques by Ibn al-Farid (Institut Français d'Etudes Arabe de Damas); 36 Abu Firas Chevalier poète by Abu Firas al-Hamdani (Publisud); 42 Al ashikha al-moutasawfa, Dar Tallas by Rabi'a al-'Adawiyya; 44 L'homme et la mer, Les fleurs du mal by Charles Baudelaire; 48 Pir Sultan Abdal; 52 Anthologie Hïkus by Yosa Buson; 54 Rubiyat by Omar Khayyam; 56 La liberté, La légende des siècles by Victor Hugo; 58 The Rose Garden by Saadi; 62, 74, 80, 82, 88, 90, 96, 118 from Desert Songs of the Night edited by Suheil Bushrui and James M. Malarkey (Saqi Books); 68 The Prophet by Kahlil Gibran; 70 Macbeth (V, 5) by William Shakespeare; 76 Poems, Book 1 by John Keats; 86 Auguries of Innocence by William Blake; 100 Second Faust by Johann Wolfgang von Goethe; 102 Ibn Khafâdja l'Andalou (Editions El-Ouns); 104 Diwan by Abu al-Attahia; 108 Abu al-Qasim al-Shabbi (Société Tunisienne de Diffusion); 110 Anthologie de la poésie persane by Urfi Shirazi; 126 Le Lac, Méditations poétiques by Alphonse de Lamartine.